W9-AOP-708

Coastlines
of the
CARIBBEAN

This volume is part of a series of volumes on
Coastlines of the World. The papers included
in the volume are to be presented at
Coastal Zone '91.

Volume Editor Gillian Cambers
Series Editor Orville T. Magoon

Published by the
American Society of Civil Engineers
345 East 47th Street
New York, New York 10017-2398

ABSTRACT

This proceedings, *Coastlines of the Caribbean,* contains papers presented at Coastal Zone '91, the Seventh Symposium on Coastal and Ocean Management held in Long Beach, California, July 8-13, 1991. This volume is part of a continuing series of volumes of *Coastlines of the World.* Some of the topics covered include environmental considerations, engineering and science; data gathering, and monitoring; legal, regulatory, and political aspects of coastal management; planning, conservation, and development; and public information and citizen participation. This volume provides the professionals, decision-makers, and the general public with a broad understanding of these subjects as they relate to the Caribbean.

Library of Congress Cataloging-in-Publication Data

Symposium on Coastal and Ocean Management (7th: 1991: Long Beach, Calif.)
    Coastlines of the Caribbean/volume edited by Gillian Cambers.
       p.   cm.—(Coastlines of the world)
    "These papers were presented at Coastal Zone '91, the Seventh Symposium on Coastal and Ocean Management, held in Long Beach, California, July 8-12, 1991"—T.p. verso.
    Includes indexes.
    ISBN 0-87262-836-1
    1. Coasts—Caribbean Area—Congresses. 2. Coastal zone management—Caribbean Area—Congresses. I. Cambers, Gillian. II. Title. III. Series.
    GB459.17.S96   1991
    333.91'7'09729—dc20   91-4236
                                      CIP

FOREWORD

Coastal Zone '91, is the seventh in a series of multidisciplinary biennial symposia on comprehensive coastal and ocean management. Professionals, citizens and decision makers met for five days in Long Beach, California, to exchange information and views on matters ranging from regional to international scope and interest. This year's theme was entitled "A SPOTLIGHT ON SOLUTIONS, GLOBAL CONCERNS: MULTI-LEVEL RESPONSIBILITIES", emphasized a recurrent focus on practical coastal problem solving.

Sponsors and affiliates included the American Shore and Beach Preservation Association, American Society of Civil Engineers (ASCE), Coastal Zone Foundation, Department of Commerce, National Oceanic and Atmospheric Administration, as well as many other organizations (see title page). The range of sponsorship hints at the diversity of those attending the Coastal Zone '91 Symposium. The presence of these diverse viewpoints will surely stimulate improved coastal and ocean management through the best of current knowledge and cooperation.

This volume of the "Coastlines of the World" series is included as part of the Coastal Zone '91 Conference. The purpose of this special regional volume is to focus on the coastline and coastal zone managment of the Caribbean.

Each volume of the "Coastlines of the World" series has one or more guest volume editors representing the particular geographical or topical area of interest.

All papers have been accepted for publication by the Volume Editors. All papers are eligible for discussion in the Journal of Waterway, Port, Coastal, and Ocean Engineering, ASCE and all papers are eligible for ASCE awards.

An eighth conference is now being planned to maintain this dialogue and information exchange. Information is available by contacting the Coastal Zone Foundation, P.O. Box 279, Middletown, California 95461, U.S.A.

Orville T. Magoon
Coastlines of the World
Series Editor

PREFACE

The Caribbean is a very diverse and complex region. The countries surrounding the Caribbean Sea include the northern countries of South America, several Central American countries and several island chains stretching in broad arcs from Central America to South America. The Caribbean Sea is closely linked with the Gulf of Mexico and the Straits of Florida. Thus the geographical term "Caribbean" includes all these countries. This volume, however, deals not with the entire region, but with the chains of islands including the Greater and Lesser Antilles and the Bahamas chain.

Many of the islands are small and partly because of this, the coastal zone takes on additional importance to that of larger countries. In most islands the coastal zone is intensively used and is the focus for the major residential, commercial, industrial, and tourist developments. The importance of coastal tourism to these island states cannot be overstressed, in some islands it is the major industry. Thus sound and effective management of the coastal zone is of the greatest importance to the Caribbean Islands.

While many of the islands do not have specific CZM agencies, most islands are trying to find solutions to their coastal problems in a variety of ways. There is a nucleus of qualified and experienced persons in the region who are attempting to deal with a vast array of coastal problems. This volume is testimony to that statement, however, it is recognized that the number of persons is small and the budgets devoted to CZM in the region.

Many of the papers in this volume deal with specific aspects of CZM or problems eg. beach sand mining, pollution, coastal erosion, public access. Indeed much of the work being done in the Caribbean Islands is of an empirical and applied nature and is essentially problem oriented. This is perhaps inevitable within developing countries. The papers in this section have been ordered so as to progress from a general approach dealing with several islands to a specific problem approach dealing with individual islands. The final papers in this volume show the results of some more theoretical research work that is being conducted within institutions both inside and outside the region. It is anticipated that a combination of the two approaches and a sharing of information will lead to the effective management of the coastal zones of the Caribbean Islands.

The Caribbean Islands form a part of an interesting region, one of the most varied and diverse within the developing world. The management of these coastal zones provides an exciting challenge for the future. It is hoped that this volume will encourage further interest and work in the region, the CZM challenges must be met before the Caribbean Islands can achieve their goal of sustainable development.

Dr. Gillian Cambers
Volume Editor

CONTENTS

INTERNATIONAL CZM:
SMALL ISLAND STATES/ARCHIPELAGOS

PUBLIC ACCESS

POLLUTION AND CONTROL STUDIES
AND STRATEGIES I

ECONOMICS AND SOCIAL SCIENCE

CORAL REEFS AND SURF ZONES

OCEAN MANAGEMENT TECHNIQUES AND EXPERIENCES

COASTAL PROCESSES II

COASTLINES OF TRINIDAD AND TOBAGO
A COASTAL STABILITY PERSPECTIVE

Diane Bertrand,[1] Charmaine O'Brien-Delpesh[1]
Lloyd Gerald,[1] Hayden Romano[1]

Abstract

The Institute of Marine Affairs embarked as early as 1982 on coastal conservation studies and a structured programme of data collection and analysis was established from 1985. Forty-one beach profile stations have been established around Trinidad and Tobago. The nearshore processes and beach profile data collected at these stations indicate that the complex interplay of the aspect, coastal geology and the nearshore hydrodynamics contribute to the form of the coastlines.

The south coast of Trinidad is one of the more dynamic coastlines. The geological outcrops of this coast consist mainly of weak unconsolidated silts, clays and sandstones which provide little resistance to the oncoming waves.

The geological formations exposed along the east and west coasts of Trinidad are similar. The difference in the degree of coastal erosion experienced along these coasts is primarily due to the fact that the west coast is sheltered whilst the east is open to the Atlantic Ocean and therefore to direct attack by high energy waves. The highly indented north coast with its sheltered inlets is composed of low grade metamorphic rocks. These resistant rocks and the inherent geomorphology are the major factors responsible for the stability of this coastline.

Tobago has had a different geological history from Trinidad. The northeastern two-thirds of the island is

[1]Institute of Marine Affairs, P.O. Box 3160, Carenage Post Office, Carenage, Trinidad and Tobago, West Indies.

composed of igneous and metamorphic rocks whereas the
southwestern third consists of coralline limestone. This
distribution of geology has influence the nature of Tobago's
coastlines. The coralline region is less rugged and indented
than the other region.

Introduction

Trinidad and Tobago, the most southerly of the Caribbean
islands are 5,128 km^2 in area and have a population of 1.2
million (Fig. 1). The rapid rate and extent of coastal
development along the 670 km of the islands' coastlines have
warranted that comprehensive and systematic coastal
conservation studies be conducted.

The Institute of Marine Affairs (IMA) has, from 1982
been involved in coastal erosion studies and in 1985 a
systematic method of coastal data collection and monitoring
was established. Previous workers have examined isolated
sections of the coastlines to assess specific problems.
(Deane, 1971, 1973; Bachew et al 1983, Georges et al 1983;
Georges, 1984, Hudson et al 1984). This paper is an analysis
of the coastlines of Trinidad and Tobago, using the data
obtained from IMA's monitoring studies.

Methodology

Beach profile and nearshore processes data from 1985 to
1990 were analysed for 18 of the 41 IMA beach stations around
Trinidad and Tobago. Generally data was collected quarterly
from 1985-1989 and monthly from 1990. The 1990 data was used
to calculate the averages for breaker height, wave period and
longshore current speeds and directions. These values were
compared with the data from the preceding years to indicate
seasonal and spatial trends. The 18 beach stations selected
were tied into the national bench marks established by the
Lands and Surveys Division (Figs. 2 & 3). Sweep zones for
the period August 1989 to 1990 were compared for eight bays
around the islands and the horizontal distance of the
foreshore – mean sea level (msl) intercept from the bench
mark station was calculated. Foreshore slopes were
calculated and analysed for seasonal trends and storm events

Description of Study Area
Climate

Trinidad and Tobago experiences a humid tropical climate
(mean annual temp. of 25.7^{o}). Rainfall varies widely over
short distances and is both relief and convectional in

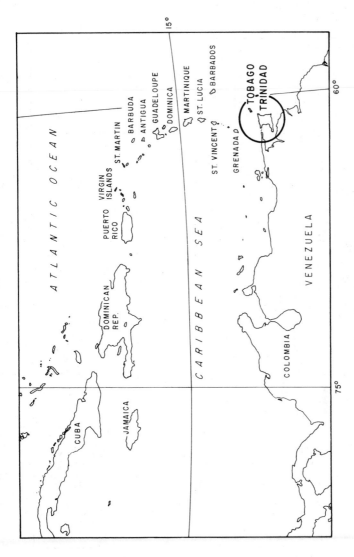

Fig. I. Location Map Of Trinidad and Tobago West Indies.

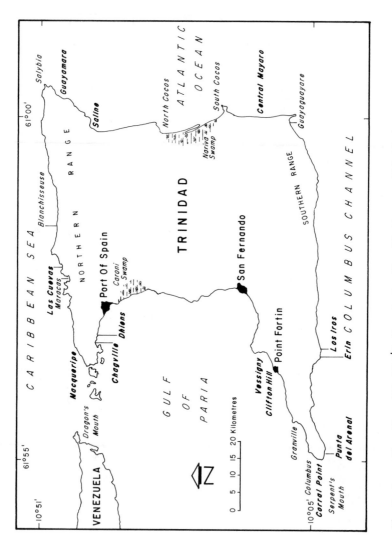

Fig. 2   Location Map Of IMA'S Beach Profile Stations — Trinidad.

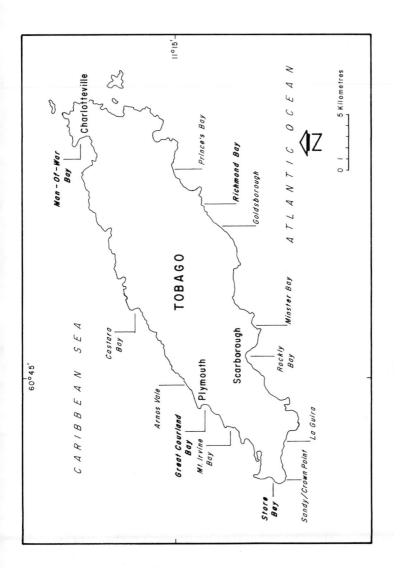

Fig.3 Location Map Of IMA'S Beach Profile Stations — Tobago.

origin. The prevailing wind system is the Northeast Trades and the dominant wind direction is from the north-east in the dry season, (December to May) and from the east in the wet season, (May to December). Wind speeds average approximately 11-30 km/h. The official hurricane season extends from June to November with August and September being the most active periods. Trinidad and Tobago, although located south of what is defined as the Atlantic Hurricane Zone, occasionally experience hurricanes, tropical storms, and the accompanying coastal conditions.

Currents

The Guyana current is the major ocean current influencing the islands. As it reaches Trinidad, this northward flowing current divides into westward and northward components. The western current flows through the Columbus Channel on Trinidad's south coast entering the Gulf of Paria through the Serpent's Mouth. In the Gulf of Paria the flow is in a general northerly direction. A clockwise eddy occurs near the middle of the Gulf. The northward flowing component of the Guyana Current moves along the east coast of Trinidad and flows through the Tobago Sound, the channel which separates Trinidad from Tobago. This current also continues towards the northeast along the south coast of Tobago. (van Andel and Postma, 1954).

Tides

The tidal regime experienced is a function of tide waves from both the Caribbean Sea and the Atlantic Ocean (Gade, 1961). The tide is described as mixed, with a predominantly semi-diurnal influence. The maximum tidal range is 1.3 metres. (Edwards, 1983).

Geomorphology

Trinidad's coastlines can be subdivided geographically into north, south, east and west and Tobago's coastlines into north, south and southwest. Trinidad's north coast is located along the foothills of the deeply dissected east-west trending Northern Range. This range is a complex folded and faulted region with beds dipping steeply $(30 - 70^{\circ})$ to the south (Potter, 1977). Lithologically the range consists of low grade regionally metamorphosed crystalline limestone, phyllites, mica-schists and quartzites(Kugler, 1959). On Trinidad's rocky north coast, the rock faces are steep and usually thickly forested. Proceeding west to east along the north coast the relief decreases and the coast becomes less rugged (Georges, 1983). The northern coastline is open to the Caribbean Sea and also to the direct influence of the Northeast Trade Winds.

The east coast is rugged in its northern section where the rocks from the Northern Range outcrop. Further south the coastline becomes gentler, where in the central regions the Nariva wetlands are found. South of the wetlands low cliffs outcrop.

The south coast is backed by steep cliffs which occur in the dominant sandstone lithologies of the Southern Range. Within the sandstone units subordinate lenses and bands of silt, clay and siltstone occur (Kugler, 1959).

The geomophology of the west coast is very similar to that of the east. It is rocky and rugged in the northern section, giving way to low swamp land in its midsection. In the south, low and medium cliffs of sandstones, clays and siltstones outcrop along the coastline. (Georges, 1983).

Tobago's coastline may be generally described as rocky and rugged. The metamorphic and volcanic rocks which cover the northeastern two-thirds of the island is steeper and more irregular producing a highly indented coastline. The south western region of the island which consists of a limestone platform although embayed is less rugged.

Results

The wave period trends for the 18 beach profile stations (Jan – Dec 1990) are illustrated in Figure 4. The following are the trends observed:
i.   The north coasts of both Trinidad and Tobago show high mean wave periods. (6.6 and 8.9 secs).
ii   Trinidad's south coast exhibits large ranges (1.1–14.0 secs) while the wave periods on the west coast are shorter. (2.0–11.1 secs).
iii   Chagville, on the west coast has the lowest range (2.2–3.5 secs) and mean (2.6 secs) of all the stations studied.

Figure 5 is a summary of the breaker height data for the 18 profile stations around Trinidad and Tobago (Jan. – Dec. 1990). Overall trends indicated that,
i.   Breaker heights on the north coast of Trinidad increased eastward.
ii.   Guayamara on the northeast coast of Trinidad experiences the highest wave energy (max. breaker height 1.5 m).
iii.   Low breaker height readings (0.25 m)were recorded at Saline on the east coast when compared with the other two bays on this coastline.

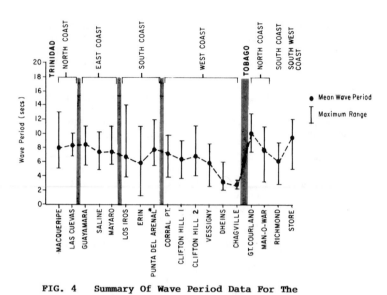

FIG. 4   Summary Of Wave Period Data For The
18 Beach Profile Stations (Jan.–Dec. 1990)

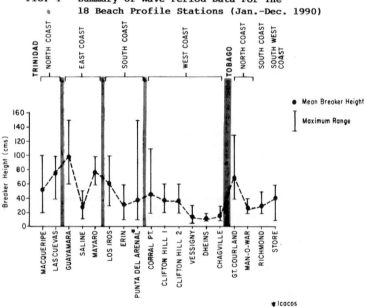

FIG. 5   Summary Of Breaker Height Data For The
18 Beach Profile Stations (Jan.–Dec. 1990)

iv. South coast bays experience moderate breaker heights
     (0.1-1.5 m) while west coast bays have the lowest
     energy breakers (0.05-1.1 m).
v.   In Tobago, Great Courland on the north coast exhibits
     the highest breaker heights (max. breaker height 1.3 m)
     with the other bays, Man of War on the north coast,
     Richmond on the south coast and Store Bay on the
     southwest experiencing moderate breaker heights (0.1-
     0.6 m).

     Longshore current data (Fig. 6) analysed for the 18
beach stations (Jan - Dec 1990) indicated that:
i.   Two longshore directions were observed at all stations
     except Saline and Clifton Hill(Profile 2) in Trinidad
     and Richmond in Tobago.
ii. The north, east and south coasts of Trinidad experience
     the most diversity in current velocities.
iii. Longshore velocities are highest at Saline Bay (16.0-
     52.1 cm/sec) on the east coast and at Los Iros (3.5-
     63.3 cm/sec) and Erin on the south coast.

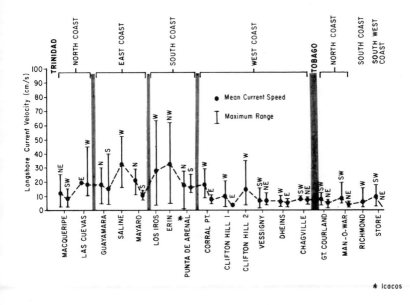

FIG. 6   Summary Of Longshore Current Velocity Data
          For the 18 Beach Profile Stations (Jan.-Dec. 1990)

iv. Tobago's coastlines (2.0-9.7 cm/sec) along with
     Trinidad's west (3.2-15.5 cm/sec) coast have the
     weakest longshore currents.

     Spatial and seasonal variations in wave energy, (i.e.,
breaker heights) for the coastlines of Trinidad and Tobago
are identified on Fig. 7 using data from 1985 to 1990.

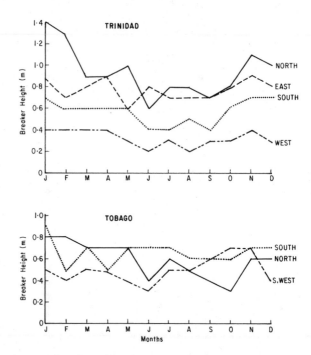

**FIG. 7   Mean Monthly Breaker Heights Along
            Trinidad And Tobago's Coastlines (1985-1990)**

The following trends can be identified.

i.   The north coast of Trinidad has the highest wave energy which decreases along the east, south and west coasts. Similarly, in Tobago the north coast experiences the highest wave energy.

ii. Wave energy increases from November to February, (winter period) on all coasts.

iii. Between July to September (summer period) another high is recorded.

Table 1 summarises the results from the littoral data.

TABLE 1 - SUMMARY OF LITTORAL DATA - TRINIDAD & TOBAGO (1990)

	MEAN BREAKER HT. (m)	RANGE (m)	MEAN WAVE PERIOD (Secs)	RANGE (Secs)	LONGSHORE CURRENT DIRECTION
TRINIDAD					
N. Coast	0.65	0.2 - 1.1	6.6	5.0 - 13.0	NE + SW E + W
E. Coast	0.68	0.1 - 1.5	7.7	4.8 - 11.0	N + S W
S. Coast	0.41	0.1 - 1.5	6.7	1.1 - 14.0	W, NW, N + S
W. Coast	0.25	0.5 - 1.1	5.0	2.0 - 11.1	E + W SW + NE
TOBAGO					
N. Coast	0.5	0.2 - 1.3	8.9	3.2 - 12.9	SW, NE
S. Coast	0.3	0.2 - 0.5	6.15	2.9 - 8.8	W
S.W. Coast	0.4	0.1 - 0.6	9.3	5.0 - 12.1	SW + NE

Sweep zones illustrated in Figures 8a and b show the temporal and spatial variability of beach profiles. Wide sweep zones are characteristic of high energy beaches, for example Las Cuevas, Guayamara, Mayaro and Great Courland. These bays also undergo rapid beach change or a high degree of beach mobility, and exhibit steep foreshore slopes (5.0° - 21.8°). The msl foreshore intercept calculated for the high mobility beaches display progradation during the summer and recession during the winter. Foreshore slope data showed no discernable trends. Narrow sweep zones were found to be characteristic of bays which are sheltered and experiences low wave energy (Macqueripe and Chagville, Fig. 8b). These bays also have relatively low to moderate foreshore slopes (2.6° to 6°).

Discussion

Broad trends can be identified along the coastlines of Trinidad and Tobago based on location and littoral processes. The profile data reveals more specific characteristics. On the north coast, the aspect makes it directly vulnerable to waves generated by the Northeast

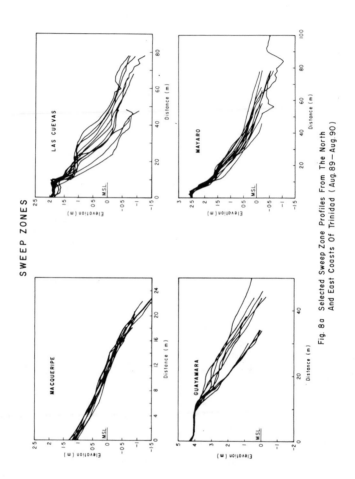

Fig. 8a   Selected Sweep Zone Profiles From The North
And East Coasts Of Trinidad (Aug. 89 — Aug. 90)

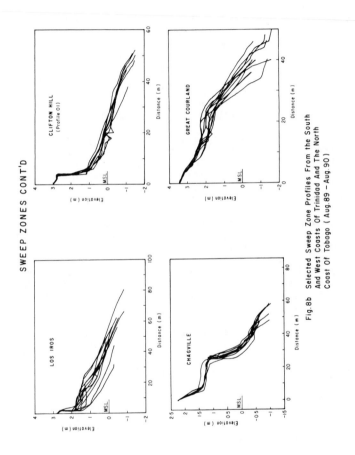

SWEEP ZONES CONT'D

Fig. 8b   Selected Sweep Zone Profiles From the South
And West Coasts Of Trinidad And The North
Coast Of Tobago (Aug. 89 – Aug. 90)

Trades.   This high energy coast has weak to moderate
longshore currents due to the direct approach of the waves.
The very narrow sweep zone at Macqueripe contrasts to the
wider zone at Las Cuevas which is a more open bay with a
more north facing aspect than Macqueripe.

The east coast displays a decrease in energy from
Guayamara to Mayaro.   Guayamara is open to the Atlantic
Ocean and receives direct wave attack from the east.   As
such, its wave energy is high and it has a very dynamic
foreshore slope. Longshore velocities are also high. This
high degree of beach mobility suggests that there is a
large sediment supply available to Guayamara and Mayaro.
Saline, because of its southeast facing aspect, its
offshore reefs and its prominent headlands does not
illustrate the characteristic east coast dynamics.

The oblique wave approach on the south coast produces
moderate to high longshore current speeds. The south coast
experiences moderate breaker heights because it is
relatively sheltered compared to the east coast.   The south
coast exhibits short and long period waves because the
waves are both wind generated and affected by ocean swells.

Based on field observations and supported by previous
workers the bays at the southern section of the west coast
are high energy and more dynamic than the bays on the
northern section of this coastline.   Corral Point and
Clifton Hill experience cliff recession, while Vessigny and
Dheins Bay appear to be relatively stable bays. Chagville
which is a man made beach shows signs of erosion due to the
lack of beach nourishment.

Tobago Bays generally show a similar littoral
characteristics to Trinidad.   Tobago's coastline is
generally exposed. As such the wave energy is directly
related to the aspect of the bay.

Conclusion
i.   Littoral data showed broad trends especially in terms
     of energy along the coastlines.   In the case of
     profile data, it was difficult to identify broad
     trends because of the limited data.

ii. Beach mobility is directly related to the increase in
     wave energy which occurs during the winter swells and
     tropical storms and hurricanes.

iii. Further work needs to be done to obtain a better
     understanding of the coastlines of Trinidad and
     Tobago. Offshore bathymetry, sea level rise studies,
     tectonics, sediment budget and aerial photography work

will aid in this advancement.

Acknowledgements
The authors would like to thank the management and staff of the Institute of Marine Affairs especially Mr. Anthony Cummings and Mr. Rodney Ramkissoon for the illustrations and Ms. Maylene Croney and Ms. Cheryl King for typing the manuscript. Special mention must be made to the Geological Technicians, Mr. Peter Joseph and Mr. Jerome Chuckaree without whose contribution this work would not have been completed.

References

Bachew, S., Hudson, D., and Gerald, A., (1983). Analysis of the coastal problems at Los Iros Bay, Trinidad, West Indies. Transactions of the 10th Caribbean Geological Conference, Cartagena, Colombia. 20p.

Bachew, S., and Lewis, N., (1985). Impacts of beach sand mining at Goldsborough Bay, Tobago. Transactions of the 1st Geological Conference, Geological Society of Trinidad and Tobago, Port-of-Spain, Trinidad. 21p.

Deane, Compton, (1971). Coastal erosion – Point Fortin to Los Gallos. Second Interim Report. Government of Trinidad and Tobago, Ministry of Planning and Development and Ministry of Works. 30p.

Deane, Compton, A.W., (1973). Coastal erosion – Point Fortin to Los Gallos. Vol. 1. Final Report. Government of Trinidad and Tobago, Ministry of Planning and Development and Ministry of Works.

Edwards, K., (1983). Preliminary description of currents in the nearshore waters of the Gulf of Paria – Northwest Peninsula area, Chaguaramas. Institute of Marine Affairs, Chaguaramas. 129p.

Gade, H.G., (1961). "On some oceanographic observations in the southeastern Caribbean sea and the adjacent Atlantic ocean with special reference to the influence of the Orinoco River." Boletin Instituto Oceanographico Universidad de Oriente, Venezuela Vol. 1., No. 2. pp287-312.

Georges, C., (1983). Coastal classification for Trinidad. Institute of Marine Affairs, Chaguaramas. 10p.

Georges, C., (1984). Impacts of beach sand mining at Turtle Beach, Great Courland Bay, Tobago. Institute of Marine Affairs, Chaguaramas. 28p.

Georges, C., Greenidge, B., and Hudson, D., (1983). Beach
    sediments of Trinidad, West Indies. Transactions of
    the 10th Caribbean Geological Conference, Cartagena,
    Colombia. 26p.

Hudson, D. and Bachew, S., (1984). Coastal erosion
    problems, Southern Trinidad. Institute of Marine
    Affairs, Chaguaramas. 10p.

Kugler, H.G. (1959). Geological Map of Trinidad. Orel
    Fursli Arts Graphiques, S.A. Zurich (Switzerland).

Potter, H.C., (1977). The overturned anticline of the
    Northern Range of Trinidad near Port-of-Spain. Jour.
    Geol. Soc. Lond., V. 129, pt. 2, pp133-138.

van Andel, Tj., and Postma, H.,(1954). Recent Sediments of
    the Gulf of Paria: Reports of the Orinoco Shelf
    Expedition, Vol. 1. North Holland Publishing Company,
    Amsterdam, 240p.

FACING MANAGEMENT CHALLENGES ON THE BARBADOS
COASTLINE: The Problem of Coastline Accesses

Atherley K. A., Nurse L. A., and Toppin Y. B.[1]

ABSTRACT

The problem of providing appropriate and safe public access to the coastline is one that has been confronting coastal zone managers and planners in Barbados for the last 20 years. Despite the presence of some 58 access points, there have been numerous complaints about the inadequate nature of the accesses, particularly with respect to quality of services and facilities. Issues relating to ownership of dry beach lands, land owners' assumption of ownership of artificially created beach lands, the public's misuse of rights-of-way over private land, and the threats to increased de facto 'privatization' of beaches as coastline development continues, all speak to the need for a strategic approach to coastline access management. Such a strategy can be integrated into an overall coastal zone management policy, having the essential ingredients of sound planning, namely the identification and development of existing accesses, the acquisition of new access space, and the relevant legislative reform. Set within a multiple use framework to coastal planning, these tasks appear to be attainable.

1. INTRODUCTION

The present pattern of land use within Barbados' coastal zone is largely the product of socio-economic policies since the island assumed Independence from British rule in 1966.

Historically, all lands including the coastal lands

---

[1]**Kenneth Atherley** is Coastal Planner, the Coastal Conservation Unit, Savannah Lodge, Garrison, Barbados.
Leonard Nurse is Project Manager, Coastal Conservation Unit, Savannah Lodge, Garrison, Barbados.
Yolanda Toppin is Senior Town Planner, Town and Country Planning Office, Block B, Garrison, Barbados.

were a part of an active sugar cane plantation system.
Beach lands were easily accessible to all, as there was no
intensive building development. The population lived in
clusters throughout the island, primarily inland in the
vicinity of prime agricultural land. However, following
emancipation from slavery in 1838, the later evolution of
free villages and the gradual diversification of commercial
activities, there was initial development in the coastal
zone. The passing of the Public Health Act 1908 brought the
administration of general land use policy under the
authority of the Board of Health.

With Independence came a new thrust to diversify the
island's mono-crop economy. The late 1960s saw the
introduction of an agricultural land use policy which
permitted the subdivision of large plantations[2] into 10
acre, then 4 acre and eventually 2 acre lots. This
agricultural land policy had a two-fold objective: (a) to
widen the base of land ownership and (b) to give momentum
to the non-sugar diversification program (Toppin, 1982).

This period of subdivision of agricultural lands took
place at a time when high production costs, local climatic
conditions and the world market situation are considered to
have had the combined effect of reducing the role of sugar
in the island's economy between 1965 and 1976 (*Ibid.*,
1982). Sugar's contribution to Gross Domestic Product (GDP)
fell from 20% in 1965 to 7% in 1976, and brought the crop
to a level comparable with non-sugar cultivation, which
contributed 5% to GDP in 1976. The percentage of the
working population in agriculture also fell from 26.4% in
1960 to 9.5% in 1976.

This same period 1965 to 1976 saw a rapid increase in
the role of tourism in the island's economy. The passing of
the Hotel Aids Act 1967, introduced a wide range of
incentives to tourism investors, including relief from
income and other taxes, refund of customs duty, grant of
licence to import and free entry of building materials and
other items. Since 1976, tourism has become Barbados's main
income earner.

The spatial impact of the island's new emphasis in
economic policy was, the rapid physical development of
coastal lands by tourism establishments and increased
residential settlement in the coastal zone as the service

---

[2]Farms over 100 acres.

sector became the primary source of employment. These changes took place within the context of an organized physical development planning system for the island and they impacted on public accessibility to the coast.

2. PHYSICAL PLANNING IMPACTS

The first Physical Development Plan for Barbados was prepared in 1967 and published in 1970. By this time responsibility for controlling and regulating all physical development on the island rested with the Town and Country Development Planning Office (TCDPO), which was established in 1959 with interim control, and which obtained full control over the island by 1968. Development planning was mandated by the Town and Country Planning Act 1965, and in planning the best use for the island's coastal lands, consideration was obviously given to the needs of all land users. However, given the government's new economic focus, the allocation of lands adjacent to "good safe beaches" was decided "...in favour of the dollar with the highest value. "(Physical Development Plan for Barbados, 1970: 9).

Furthermore, at that time the availability of land for tourism development was considered to be more than ample, given that the 1000 acres of land on the west and south coasts which had been committed to tourism since 1964, remained undeveloped at the time of plan preparation (Ibid.).

In light of the settlement pattern in the late 1960s and the still dominant agricultural economy, the assumption of easy access by the resident population to the coast in general and beaches in particular, was not an unreasonable one. The provision of an organized beach access system was not considered an issue at the time. Unfortunately, the planners underestimated the physical impact of the Hotel Aids Act on coastal development and thus public access availability.

The release of coastal marginal lands from cultivation, the reduction in agricultural employment, the shift in population settlement towards the coastal zone for service sector employment, and the growth of tourism establishments during the 1970s, combined to result in near unbroken building development along the west and south coasts where prime beach lands are located. These processes reduced visual and in many cases physical access to the beach lands and gave rise to feelings of alienation by the resident population.

Today the use of coastal land continues to be resolved in the market place. A development planning system remains

operational, but having designated public accesses, lands
can only be legally secured for this purpose through
government acquisition. With more than 40% of the
population residing in the coastal zone, the demand for
reasonable access is increasing.

3. PREVIOUS RESEARCH

Given the nature of the development process coastal
access became an issue by the late 1970s. There have been
no less than six calls through reports for improved access
to the coast over the last 15 years. One report, Hutt
(1978) was generated through non-governmental efforts. The
Pennington (1983) report was initiated by government. The
other reports Government of Barbados (1977), Atherley
(1987), TCDPO (1987), and Atherley (1988) were prepared by
departments of government. In addition, recommendations for
improved accesses can be found in the research theses of
Nurse (1986) and Lamontagne (1987). These works all
demonstrated a need for an enhancement of quality of
accesses.

The Government of Barbados (1977), in its **Tourism
Development Plan**, stressed the need to preserve and improve
public access to all the island's coasts. The study found
that the public was not so much interested in the creation
of "numerous points" of access, but rather in an adequate
number of accesses "... convenient to their residences, of
good quality, and with desirable support facilities such as
rest rooms, snack bar, playing fields, parking areas and so
on" (p. 1v-14). Good quality beach and bathing area were
also seen to be important attributes.

The study is important not only because it sets out a
clear Government policy with respect to accesses, but also
because it identifies critical areas for acquisition and
the types of facilities required at each location.
Tragically, these proposals have not been vigorously
pursued and thus the status quo has persisted. This
highlights the apparent gap, too frequently encountered,
between useful recommendations emanating from Government
departments, and their implementation.

Hutt (*op. cit.*, 1978) represents an important survey
of beach accesses in Barbados. Concentrating on the
southeast to north coast, Hutt divided the coast into eight
segments and identified 33 access locations with varying
beach frontage widths. He also stressed the need for land
acquisition by government. Hutt recommended a phased
approach to land acquisition, with a halt to further
planning permission for commercial exploitation of the

designated sites. Hutt's proposals were not adopted as official policy by Government at the time.

In 1983, Pennington, as commissioned by government submitted a report on the establishment of a national park on the island's north to east coast. The implementation strategy included improvements to facilities at picnic sites, popular look-out points and to beaches, all appropriately sign-posted (Pennington, 1983). Government has adopted the report in principle but the national park has yet been officially declared. In the meantime the TCPO has integrated recommendations from the report into the planning process and in practice controls development along the northern and eastern coastlines to promote visual and physical access.

More recently, the CCPU in conjunction with the TCDPO studied the state of accesses in the Greater Bridgetown Area (GBA), a stretch of 16km. The report (Atherley, 1987) identified 13 existing accesses within the GBA and proposed 14 new ones which would have required land acquisition. A phased access upgrading strategy was recommended and costed over a ten year period. The recommendations were integrated into the Greater Bridgetown Physical Development Plan (GBPDP, 1987) which made proposals for acquisition at specific sites.

Nonetheless, up to five years after the GBPDP report no significant progress has come about by way of creation of new accesses. A recent check of the 14 proposed access sites revealed that one (1) has to be acquired by Government, two (2) have since been developed. The other eleven (11) sites are currently vacant, though applications have been submitted for private development at five (5) of those sites. As the development pressure continues, the public stands to lose the remaining potential accesses to the coast in the GBA.

The Barbados Physical Development Plan (Amended 1986), has incorporated the proposals of the GBPDP, and made additional recommendations for early acquisition and/or improvement of twelve sites around the island. The plan also contained recommendations for the proposed National Park area, including the provision of a system of foot-paths on the coastline, parking facilities, playing facilities and tree planting. Acquisition procedures for a few of the sites have already begun.

In 1988, bearing in mind there are constraints associated with government's acquisition process, the CCPU prepared a report (Atherley, 1988) identifying some 35 existing vehicular and pedestrian accesses along 34km of

the west and south coasts[4]. The report made specifi
recommendations on low-cost maintenance actions, includin
landscaping, sign-posting, provision of parking wher
necessary, and erection of changing facilities. Th
National Conservation Commission has begun to implemen
recommendations from these studies.

4. CURRENT STATUS OF ACCESSES

Against the background of frequent and well informe
calls for improvements to the access network in the island
it may be instructive to appraise the present quality o
these sites. Available empirical data were therefore used
supplemented by more recent field work, to survey 58 (Ma
1) recognized coastline accesses. Table 1 categorizes th
accesses by coastline stretch and on seven attribute
relating to various types of services and facilities.

4.1 Access Type and Sign-posting

Of the 58 accesses, twenty eight (48%) were classifie
as Vehicular, six (10%) as Visual, with twenty four (42%
classed as Pedestrian (Table 1). Many of the vehicula
accesses have no dedicated parking space and parking i
only possible under trees or along the road. The surve
recorded sign-posting at only five (9%) of the sites
mainly on the west coast.

4.2 Landscape Quality

Twenty seven (46%) of the 58 accesses had
predominantly natural landscape, and seven (12%) sites ha
planned landscaping. Landscaping was mixed at ninetee
(33%) sites, whereas five (9%) of the sites had n
landscaping.

4.3 Facilities and Services

Play Parks were lacking along all coastline stretche
as only four (7%) of the sites had these facilities. Twelv
(21%) of the sites were furnished with benches, an
eighteen (31%) with picnic tables. The south coast accesse
were better supplied with tables and benches than the othe
coastal stretches. Lifeguard services existed at onl

---

[4]Although on average there was 1 access per kilometer of
   coast, in reality, the accesses were poorly distribute

Map 1: LOCATION OF EXISTING ACCESSES

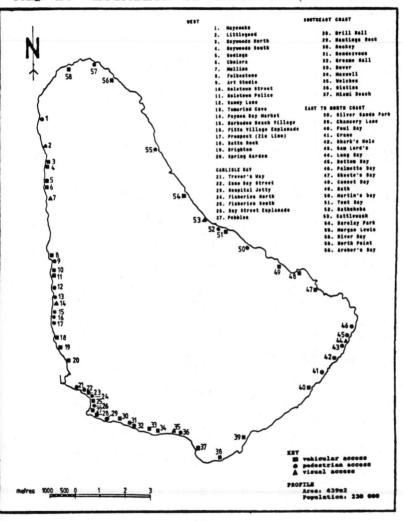

Table 1

SURVEY OF COASTLINE ACCESSES
(Barbados, 1991)

COASTAL STRETCH (No. Sites)	ACCESS TYPE			LANDSCAPE QUALITY				PLAY PARKS (No.)	TABLES AND BENCHES (No.)		LIFE-GUARD STATIONS (No.)	SIGN-POSTING (No.)	CHANGING FACILITIES (No.)
	V	Pe	Vi	N	Pl	M	No		T	B			
West (20)	10	3	7	9	2	6	3	1	1	2	6	4	5
Carlisle Bay (7)	3	0	4	0	1	5	1	1	0	3	4	1	1
South Coast (10)	5	1	4	5	3	1	1	0	6	8	4	0	3
Southeast (9)	3	1	5	5	1	3	0	1	2	2	3	0	1
East to North (12)	7	1	4	8	0	4	0	1	3	3	3	0	2
TOTAL (58)	28	6	24	27	7	19	5	4	12	18	20	5	12

NOTES: V - Vehicular Access, land with potential to hold a minimum of 5 cars.
Vi- Visual Access, track (minimum of 1m width).
Pe - Inaccessible to vehicular traffic, adjacent to coast which can carry little or no
      physical development (Window to the Sea).

N - Natural Landscape.
Pl - Planned Landscape.
M - Mixed Landscape.
No- No Adequate Landscape.
T - Tables
B - Benches

twenty (34%) of the accesses, mainly on the west and south
coasts. Only twelve (21%) sites had dedicated changing
rooms for users, again, mainly on the west and south
coasts.

5.0 CRITICAL ACCESS ISSUES

During the last 15 years the island has been
confronting a number of coastal management problems, which
though related to more general environmental, socio-
economic, and legal considerations, have had direct impacts
on the quality and quantity of coastline accesses.

5.1 Quality and Quantity

The access survey showed that though plenty in number
(58) the quality of facilities and services at coastline
accesses were inadequate. All access points should be
appropriately sign-posted. Further, it is felt that
lifeguard services should be available at all sites, as
should tables and benches. There should be more play parks
around the coastline and accesses should be landscaped
wherever necessary. It is also suggested that dedicated
parking space should be provided at sites with vehicular
access, particularly where only under-tree parking now
occurs.

The public is faced with a situation whereby, assuming
they reach an access point, there is often congestion in
the use of available facilities and services. In many
cases, desirable attributes are not present. Thus, even the
quality of the country's existing accesses is a serious
issue for recreational users of the coast.

5.2 Who really owns the beach?

The determination of those locations which afford the
public access to the coast, generally has to do with the
question, "who really owns the beach?". With the absence of
local legislation regarding ownership of beach lands,
Barbados adopts relevant Common Law positions.

At Common Law the limit of public versus private beach
lands is determined relative to High Water Mark (HWM), HWM
being the ordinary position of the tides between spring and
neap tides. Where lands abutting the HWM are privately
owned the beach lands are also private. The Crown therefore
may own beach land only if it happens to own land behind
HWM. However the Crown has indisputable claim to the
foreshore (between HWM and Low Water Mark (LWM)), and to

lands under the territorial waters of the island. Under
normal circumstances, the Crown owns the wet beach while
the dry beach is privately owned. Obviously **whosoever owns
property has a constitutional right to decide who has
access to that land and when.**Ownership of beach land
therefore becomes an issue where there is misunderstanding
or oversight of the law by private land owners, public
officers, or by the general public.

5.3 Discretionary Use

With a ten-fold increase in annual tourist arrivals
between 1960 and 1980, and with a rise in the demand for
beach space, there has also been an increase in the variety
of activities on the beaches -- an often incompatible mix
of quiet to noisy recreational and commercial activities.
The result has been greater irritation among tourists,
hotel managers, and the Barbadian public.

Beach front property owners often prefer to have
exclusive rights to the use of their own land. As Travis
observed, a major obstacle to effective beach access
programs relates to the fact that, 'people who have bought
a picture window on the sea do not like someone standing in
front of that window' (Travis, 1989, p. 4712). Therefore,
when public use of private beach land becomes a nuisance in
reality or merely by perception, the owners, having the
right to control the use of such lands, limit its use. This
results in animosity and public protest, especially in
instances when the land is owned by non-nationals. The
letters reaching the newspapers and calls to local radio
programs attest to the growing feeling of alienation among
Barbadians.

5.4 Ownership of Accreted Lands

The assumption of ownership by private landowners to
lands which have artificially or perceptibly accreted[5], has
effectively reduced public beach space in the country.
Assumption of ownership impacts on the planning process, as
demonstrated in a recent proposal to construct a large
town-house and tourist-related center, with a proposed
setback of 30m from HWM. The planning agencies observed
that the site experienced a 40m increase in beach width
between 1965 and 1985 and that studies suggested that the
accretion was rapid and perceptible (e.g Zeigler and
Anderson, 1978), due partly to structural work in the area.

---

[5]At Common Law artificially or suddenly accreted beach is
normally vested in the Crown.

It was clear that part of the development would be located on land which should have been vested in the Crown.

The matter was further complicated by the fact that the land had recently been sold and conveyed to a new owner, based on sworn surveyor's plans showing a Lot A (lands landward of the 1965 HWM position), and Lot B (beach), defined as the accreted area between the 1965 and 1985 HWM positions. The planning agencies, recognizing an area of uncertainty between private and public ownership rights to the accreted lands, referred the matter to the Attorney General's Chambers for direction.

The above example demonstrates the importance of having the ownership of accreted lands clarified as a matter of course, to ensure that both the public's rights as well as the property owner's rights are protected. While landowners have taken the initiative to periodically resurvey the beach front so as to re-establish property lines, the Crown has not asserted its rights to artificially accreted lands.

5.5 De Facto 'Privatization'

In the perception of the public, access to the coast is a right, since all beaches are presumed to be 'public'. Ironically however, some coastal sites can, in a de facto sense, become 'privatized', once property owners exercise their right to develop their land and thus deny access. It should be pointed out that the denial of public access cannot be used as the basis on which to refuse development permission. Furthermore, a refusal of permission does not impact on the ownership of the land and general control would still rest with its owners.

It is noteworthy that most of the sites which have been 'privatized' are either quality recreational zones of great scenic value, or areas where there is only one useable beach along a relatively long stretch of coast.

The problem is well illustrated by reference to two recent applications to develop lands along the northern and south-eastern coasts. In the case of the former, the applicant proposed to expand a hotel complex and subdivide adjacent lands for real estate. Effectively, the only pocket beach along the North Point coastline would have been eliminated from public use. If the proposal were approved, the only means of public access would have been via a sheer 20.0m high cliff, or alternatively by boat from the two nearest beaches at River Bay and Archer's Bay, some 3.0 km to the southeast and 2.0 km to the southwest respectively.

In the case of the proposal for the southeastern
coast, the applicant sought to subdivide 12.2 ha of land
bordering a 40.0m high cliff top. The development as
conceived, would have prevented safe public passage to the
area, arguably one of the most picturesque points along the
southeast coast. These two examples argue the need for the
urgent implementation of the acquisition process, if access
to such areas is not to become limited to the few.

5.6 Bargaining and Acquisition

There are only two procedures currently available to
coastal planners to secure land for beach access purposes.
One is public acquisition of the specified land area, the
other is to enter into an agreement with the private
developer.

The exercise of planning control through negotiation
has no legal basis under the Barbadian town planning
system. Agreements may consist, for example, of the
provision of a public beach access in exchange for a
slightly higher density than normally allowed in the
specified area. Although there is evidence that these
written agreements have worked, they are not legally
binding and do not have to be honored when there is a
change in land owners. This method is therefore totally
discretionary, and has in practice, been restricted to
situations where there is an established use right by the
resident population. The fact that developers do not have
to provide access even where a need has been identified by
the planners, is an obvious weakness in the use of this
mechanism for securing access.

The process of compulsory acquisition on the other
hand has doubtless merit. However, this procedure is
modestly used so as to minimize the perception of violation
of the rights of private property owners. Moreover,
compulsory acquisition requires compensation, which in the
context of small island economies, may limit government's
ability to expedite action.

6.0 THE MANAGEMENT CHALLENGES

With the current condition of existing accesses and
with a multitude of factors impacting on the potential for
opening new ones, it is clear that there is a need for
improvement. The challenge for effective coastal management
would be to ensure that the multiple publics have
reasonable access to most points on the coast, are fully
aware of the location of accesses, and can feel comfortable

using them, without fear of harassment (imaginary or real) from property owners. We believe that an effective access management program should contain the following:

(i) Identification and Development

Given the fact that accesses are not regularly spaced, nor have they emerged from a consciously planned policy, some are difficult to locate, others have 'uncertain status' in the perception of the public, while others are simply not known except by residents of the immediate district. A first requirement must therefore be to ensure that all access points are regularized and officially designated as such. Similarly, all designated accesses should be clearly sign-posted, bearing some logo (or other identification mark) the meaning of which can be easily understood by the public. Signs should also be erected in the most prominent location, pointing to the specific access in an unambiguous fashion.

(ii) Acquire Open Space for New Accesses

All remaining open spaces identified as critical accesses by CCPU and TCPO, must be acquired expeditiously by Government. The speed with which this process must take place cannot be over-stressed, since most of the lands so identified by Atherley (1988) and TCDPO (1988) have now been developed. This need is further underscored when one notes that of the fifty-eight (58) access points shown in Map 1, only twenty eight (48%) of them are accessible by vehicle. Vehicular accesses are insufficient and poorly organized. Compulsory acquisition is the only process which can adequately address this problem; bargaining will almost certainly only yield narrow, restricted, pedestrian rights-of-way.

(iii) Legislative Changes

Much of the disquiet about the blocking off of access to the coast, and increasing abuse of private lands by beach users can be controlled if the law is unambiguous and known to all. The same argument is applicable to private claims of ownership to public lands that have accreted artificially. Thus, there certainly is a need for clarification of common law positions on beach land ownership, on rights to accreted (or eroded) lands, and its adaptation to the Barbados situation given stated policy directives. Equally, to be effectively enforced, the legislation should be well articulated and understood by enforcers as well as the general public, including coastal land owners, surveyors, planners, and lawyers.

Furthermore, modifications to existing law should

grant authority to the appropriate government agency to
enter into agreements with developers for the purpose of
restricting or regulating development in the coastal zone
The legal authority to insist on the provision of beach
access, where desirable, should also be introduced.

7. CONCLUSION

It is important to point out that while the discussion
focuses on the problem of access _per se_, the issue can only
be satisfactorily resolved in the context of wider coastal
planning and management considerations. In other words, it
should be cautioned that the call echoed here for
implementation of an access management program, should not
be divorced from the on-going obligation to establish a
comprehensive coastal zone management plan. Indeed the
recommendations contained in this paper merely seek to
advance the latter process.

In a country where quality coastal space is limited,
the allocation of this asset must be informed by the
principle of 'multiple use'. The concept of multiple use
will help to ensure that this scarce asset is rationally
allocated among all interest groups, so that user conflict
is kept to an absolute minimum. The frequent, strident
protests from the public at the whisper of a development
which is perceived to threaten an access, are symptomatic
of user conflict.

The stated recommendations will only be implemented if
government is committed to acquisition of the necessary
coastal lands as part of an overall coastal management
program. We must move swiftly to 'redress' the imbalance in
favour of the public, though we must, at all costs, avoid
any violation of the rights of the 'other' interest group,
the property owners.

8. REFERENCES

Atherley, K. A. 1987. **"Upgrading and developing beach
     accesses in the Greater Bridgetown Region (Rendezvous
     to Holders Hill)"**. Coastal Conservation Project Unit.
     Report #5, March.

Atherley, K. A. 1988. **"Status report on existing west and
     south coast beach access (Towards low-cost
     maintenance)"**. Coastal Conservation Project Unit,
     January.

Government of Barbados, 1977. **Barbados Tourism Development**

Plan. Prepared for Ministry of Tourism and Civil Aviation.

Hotel Aids Act. 1968. In **Laws of Barbados**. Cumulative Edition. 1984. Government printing Department.

Hutt, M. B. 1978. " **'Windows to the Sea'. The Establishment of coastal facilities along south and west coast of Barbados from the Grantley Adams Airport in Christ Church to Maycocks Bay in St. Lucy"**. Report to Christian Action for Development in the Caribbean (CADEC).

Lamontagne, J. 1987. **"Coastal development in Barbados"**. M.A. Dissertation in Urban Planning, McGill University.

Nurse, L. A. 1986. **"Development and change on the Barbados Leeward Coast: A study of human impact on the littoral environment"**. PhD Dissertation, McGill University.

Pennington, N. C 1983. **"Barbados National Park"**. Report prepared for the Government of Barbados on proposals for a National park on the north and east coasts.

Toppin, Y. B. 1982. **"Agricultural land Subdivision in Barbados. 1965 - 1976"**. B.A. Dissertation. University of the West Indies. Mona Campus.

Town and Country Planning Act, 1968. In **Laws of Barbados**. Cumulative Edition. 1984. Government Printing Department.

Town and Country Development Planning Office (TCDPO), 1970. **Physical Development Plan for Barbados.** Government of Barbados.

Town and Country Development Planning Office (TCDPO), 1987. **Greater Bridgetown Physical Development Plan**. Government of Barbados.

Town and Country Development Planning Office (TCDPO), 1988. **Barbados Physical Development Plan (Amended 1986).** Government of Barbados.

Travis, W. 1989. **"Balancing the competing interests in Providing Shoreline Access"**. **Coastal Zone '89**, Vol. 4. p. 4701 - 4713.

Zeigler, J. M. and G. L, Anderson, 1978. **Barbados Coastline evaluation between Pierhead, Bridgetown and St. Lawrence Gap**. Coastal Environmental Associates, Virginia. November.

EVALUATING THE EFFICACY OF CZM IN THE EASTERN CARIBBEAN

Clement D. Lewsey, Ph.D *

Abstract

This paper will examine the importance of the coastal
zone in the Eastern Caribbean and will trace the origin
of coastal management activities in selected islands.
It will highlight the necessity for an integrated
management approach to coastal zone management and will
also explore policy initiatives for potential change in
land use controls through tax incentives, and the
incorporation of environmental indices into coastal
planning for sustainable development. The problems of
implementing coastal zone management programs in these
island nations will also be examined.

Introduction

The quest for sustainable coastal development in the
Eastern Caribbean island nations must be considered in
conjunction with the development of integrated and
coordinated coastal zone management. This approach is
mandatory because of the intensive pressure growth and
development imposes on the limited coastal zones of
these countries. The problems of managing these
intensively used areas are compounded by the conflict
between demand incentives, and the need for rational
planning and development in the coastal zone. These
measures will contribute to the long term support of
the environment and the gross domestic product of these
islands and the region as a whole.

* Clement D. Lewsey, Associate Professor, Morgan State
University. Baltimore, Maryland 21239

Initially, many coastal zone management efforts in the
Eastern Caribbean were arbitrary exercises in response
to isolated coastal problems. After further investigation, these problems continued to contribute to
effects best described as chain reactions that were
found to affect entire ecosystems, and required a
coordinated approach to identify management strategies.
This paper discusses some physical aspects of the
coastal zone in the Eastern Caribbean in relation to
major use activities associated with the area. It also
documents the effects of selected coastal land uses on
the marine environment within the Eastern Caribbean
region, and traces the origin and institutionalization
of coastal zone management efforts in selected Eastern
Caribbean countries.

This study also evaluates the bureaucratic and political
support structure in these islands to accommodate
national coastal management efforts, and makes a strong
case for the establishment of an integrated approach to
coastal zone management in order to achieve sustainable
development.

Boundary Determination

Historically, the coastal zone has been designated by
using ecological, geographical or political guidelines.
In continental maritime countries the use of watersheds
to delineate the landward limits of coastal zone boundaries have met with extensive criticism from public and
private interest groups because of the probable impact
of proposed boundaries on growth and development
activities.

In the Eastern Caribbean archipelago however, boundary
determination is of paramount importance because of the
limited geographic area of these islands, along with
the close and interrelated nature of the marine and
adjacent coastal lands. To date, coastal zone boundary
designation in the Caribbean, with regard to the landward limit, has been arbitrary based on local and/or
sectorial circumstances. For example, a 50 to 100 m.
setback was recommended for all lowland coasts in
Grenada, and a 30 m. setback was recommended for other
coasts as a result of the critical erosion problems
experienced at Gran Anse, Grenada (Cambers, 1985).

In order to overcome the problem of defining a coastal
zone boundary within such a limited area, some
researchers have suggested that in a small island
nation the entire land mass should be considered a
coastal zone. While this concept may be theoretically

feasible, its practical application is questionable
given the context of the Eastern Caribbean islands,
where incorporating the many disciplines and
governmental agencies in the coastal zone management
process is problematic, yet necessary.

Finally, the multi-jurisdictional nature of coastal
development activities on these islands has precluded
the progress of a holistic coastal zone management
concept, because of the conflicts arising from over-
lapping oversight and management responsibilities by
the relevant government ministries.

Present Uses in the Coastal Zone

Having regard to the rugged topography of most Eastern
Caribbean countries, coastal land is targeted for the
majority of development activities because of it's
accessible terrain. As a result of the demand for land,
the coastal area is home to many competing and
conflicting land use activities.

Historically, monocrop agriculture has been the major
land use activity in coastal areas, and at present still
dominates coastal land use. More recently, agriculture
has had to compete with other activities such as coastal
tourism, port facilities, industrial development, air-
ports, urbanization and local recreational activities.
However, as the competition for coastal land
intensified, agricultural activity has had to share,
and in some cases relinquish land to tourism activities
and urban development. Similarly, the competition for
beach and adjacent coastal lands between tourism,
artisanal fisheries and local recreation has skewed land
use in favor of tourism related activities. The south
and south west coast of Barbados is a typical example of
this phenomenon (Lewsey 1987).

Industrial and urban development in the coastal area
has also contributed to land and water use conflicts in
the Eastern Caribbean. There are several examples
where this development has contributed to the decline
of traditional land and water use activities. The
capital intensive industrial estate at Point Lisas in
Trinidad, while contributing to spin-off economic and
commercial activities in the region, has systematically
depleted local fishing activities. A 1989 Institute of
Marine Affairs study using the "net present value"
method, concluded that from a financial and economic
point of view, the government investment of over U.S.
$1.3 billion, when evaluated over a fifteen year period,
will result in net negative returns to the economy.

This analysis does not take into consideration the
socio-economic impacts to the many adjacent fishing
communities from the loss of their fisheries resource.
Existing high pollution levels in Kingston Harbor,
Jamaica is also indicative of intensive and competing
land and water uses in the coastal area (Wade 1985).
The traditional fisheries activity and several recreational bathing beaches at Kingston Bay have been severely
deteriorated as a result of pollution from sewage,
industrial chemicals, solid waste, including oil from
the port, heavy industrial activities and urban development that surround the bay.

Coastal Land Use and the Environment

Not withstanding the competition for land use in the
coastal area, it is instructive to assess the general
impacts of these uses on the coastal environment.
Agriculture, although a dominant land use activity in
the adjacent coastal lands, has contributed
significantly to the incidence of non-point source
pollution in the marine zone. Pesticides and
fertilizers originating from the adjacent coastal lands
and outside of this area have been transported into the
marine zone where they have had significant deleterious
effects on marine ecosystems. Fish kills and coral reef
stress are typical examples of the impact from
agricultural areas in several Eastern Caribbean
countries.

The prognosis of this phenomena is that agricultural
chemicals will continue to accumulate throughout the
marine environment, and will impact heavily on the
artisanal fishing industry, the food chain, and coral
reefs. Furthermore, these events will impact on the
stability of the beaches and the well being of coastal
user groups such as recreational bathers, tourists and
artisanal fishermen.

Extensive research has been done on tourism development
and its impact on the Caribbean environment. Specific
examples in Grenada (Archer, 1984), St. Lucia (Tole,
1985) and Barbados (Proctor & Redfern International,
1984) show a direct relationship between coastal
tourism development, coastal pollution, and erosion.
In the beach erosion study at Gran Anse, Grenada,
Cambers and Archer concluded that the extensive
incidence of coastal erosion at Gran Anse was partially
the result of pollution from tourist facilities which
contributed to the denudation of the off shore reef
system, and the resulting exposure of the beach area to
more intensive wave energy.

A sequential air photo analysis of the west and southwest coasts of Barbados (Lewsey, 1978) showed
significant reduction in size of the fringe reef system
of the southwest coast of the island as a result of
tourism related development. This study also suggested
that the fringe reef systems on the west coast was being
threatened from sewage and waste pollution as a result
of tourism development. Cambers in her 1987 report
documented serious erosion taking place along the west
coast of Barbados for the past 30 years. It should be
noted that the reduction of the fringe reef systems on
the west coast of Barbados is not only the result of the
deteriorating water quality, but also because of the
practice of dynamiting fringe reef areas to create nearshore sandy bathing pools for hotel guests.

Congruent with tourism, coastal urbanization and
industrial development have contributed significantly
to the degradation of the marine environment. In many
Eastern Caribbean countries upwards of 70% of the
population live and work in the coastal area. For
example, 88% of the population of Trinidad lives on the
west coast while 93% of the labor force is employed in
the same area. This coastal area is also home to a large
industrial estate which accommodates an iron and steel
smelter, ammonia based fertilizer plants and an
electricity generating power plant along with other
minor spinoff industries. This 80 mile stretch of coast
also accommodates several multi-purpose and specialized
ports, the two largest urban centers and four other
urban growth areas. In addition, there are two oil
refineries, a plethora of off shore oil exploration and
drilling platforms, and several minor industrial estates
with activities including rum distillation, metal
fabrication, petrochemical production and textiles. It
also should be noted that 60% of the country's fish
catch is landed on this west coastal area.

The cumulative impact of these multi purpose land/water
use activities have had a significant impact on the
water quality of the Gulf of Paria. This water body
simulates an estuarine type environment and is very
shallow, measuring 70 fathoms at its deepest point. The
environmental legacy of intense development activity on
the west coast area of Trinidad has resulted in periodic
fish kills, the elimination of shell fish beds, the
pollution of recreational bathing beaches, and the high
toxic residues found in the remaining shell and fin fish
populations. Variations of Trinidad's west coast
development experience can be identified along the west
and southwest coast of Barbados, and in Kingston Harbor,
Jamaica.

Exploring the Regional Origin of Coastal Zone Management

Coastal Zone Management may be defined as a "dynamic process in which a coordinated strategy is developed and implemented for the allocation of environmental, socio-cultural, and institutional resources to achieve the conservation and sustainable multiple use of the coastal zone" (CAMPNET 1989). This definition suggests four major preemptive considerations, they are:

1)   the process must be dynamic to meet the demands of a constantly changing coastal environment and the management strategy must be flexible to accommodate these changes;
2)   a coordinated and integrated program must be established to accommodate the interest of diverse groups and agencies in an efficient manner;
3)   the program must reflect a capability to allocate environmental, socio-cultural and institutional resources in order to apportion and balance the broad spectrum of natural and human resources; and,
4)   the strategic program must protect, preserve and enhance the coastal zone in order to achieve sustainable multiple use of the area.

These considerations reference the need for coastal zone management to be a flexible process, that requires the integrated input of several governmental and non-governmental organizations (NGO) working in tandem, to achieve sustainable development while preserving and maintaining the environmental integrity of the coastal area.

Several Eastern Caribbean nations have initiated aspects of coastal zone management to address their specific environmental concerns. In the case of Barbados three major factors contributed to the establishment of a coastal zone management program, they were:

1)   severe erosion along the west and southwest coast because of the destruction of fringe reefs caused by poor water quality;
2)   seasonal fluctuations in sea swells caused by storm surge and hurricanes, and to a lesser extent, sea level rise; and,
3)   the high incidence of poorly placed sea defense structures to protect private property along the coast.

The Barbados coastal zone management effort, called the Coastal Conservation Unit, was initiated in 1984 pursuant to a study by a team of Canadian consultants. It's major tasks were to:

1)   monitor on a regular basis beach changes, waves,
currents and tides;
2)   advise coastal users on all sea defense structures,
including the modification of existing structures and
the design of new structures;
3)   advise and on all new developments in the coastal
zone in collaboration with the Town and Country
Planning Office; and,
4)   advise and liaise with other government agencies
wherever necessary on all matters pertaining to coastal
construction and development (Cambers, 1987).

The Coastal Conservation Unit also undertakes research
studies in benthic and water quality surveys, coastal
processes, and reef studies. The Unit provides on the
job training to government officials from other Eastern
Caribbean countries.

In the case of Grenada, a study by Jackson et. al, in
1983 (A Physical Tourism Development Plan), identified
beach erosion as a major problem at Gran Anse Bay,
where measurements taken over a two year period from
1970 - 1972 showed erosion rates of 2 meters per year.
A subsequent Organization of American States (OAS) study
in 1984 identified the major causes of erosion at Gran
Anse to be similar to those found on the west and south
west coasts of Barbados. They included:

1)   natural phenomena such as hurricanes, winter
swells, possible sea level rise, and/or land subsidence;
2)   poor water quality, that was linked to coastal reef
stress north of Gran Anse; and,
3)   extensive beach sand mining conducted at Gran Anse.

As a result of these findings, the government of Grenada
and the OAS launched a Coastal Monitoring Program in
August 1985. The major objectives of this monitoring
program were to periodically measure beach profiles at
Gran Anse and other designated beaches; to measure wave
energy and surface currents in the Gran Anse area; and,
monitor possible sea level rise.

After the first year, the program expanded to include
water quality monitoring, while quantitative reef
surveying was scheduled for the future. A 50 meter
development setback policy was also recommended to
regulate coastal development in fragile areas. The
implementation of such a setback policy however, would
require integrated and cooperative efforts between the
Coastal Monitoring Program, Grenada's Development
Control Authority and the Town & Country Planning
Agency. This Coastal monitoring program is also

expected to have direct input into resolving the
island's erosion problems caused by coastal sand mining.
Clearly, the activities in Barbados and Grenada may be
viewed as the early stages of the development of an
integrated coastal management program.

An alternate mechanism was used to respond to years of
extensive coastal erosion along the west and north
coasts of the island of Nevis. This strategy, spear-
headed by the Nevis Historical and Conservation Society
(a local NGO) involved citizen participation that
influenced the government's decision to initiate
coastal management activities. This society encouraged
the government to study the causes and extent of beach
erosion along its coastal areas. The results of the
study showed that sections of Pinneys beach had eroded
at a rate of 1 meter per year over a thirty year period
(Cambers 1983). The study also determined that the
causes of erosion were primarily as a result of both
natural phenomena and beach sand mining, and recommended
a setback of 100 meters from the high water mark for all
new buildings on low lying coastal lands.

The government of Nevis responded to the findings by
establishing a 37m. buffer zone from the high water mark
where no buildings would be permitted. For major
institutional buildings and hotels, a 91m. setback from
the high water mark along with a maximum building
height of 90m. was also recommended (Corker 1988).

It should be noted that although these recommendations
are still provisional, they are being enforced by the
Nevis Town & Country Planning Agency. For example,
these setback guidelines were incorporated into the
citing of a major 200 room hotel behind Pinneys beach
in 1989 (Cambers 1983). The effectiveness of these land
use controls were tested in September 1989 when
hurricane Hugo passed within 60 miles of the island of
Nevis. Although the island experienced severe erosion
along its coasts as a result of the storm, the
utilization of a setback policy clearly contributed to
the protection of the new hotel. The remaining buffer
zone also provided adequate reserves to allow the beach
to re-nourish itself.

Although the erosion problems experienced in Nevis
certainly contributed to the formulation of a successful
coastal management partnership experience between
government and the private sector, the problem of
extensive sand mining still needs to be addressed and
resolved through a process of integrated coastal
management. While it has been established that natural

phenomena is the primary cause of coastal erosion in
Nevis, sand mining continues to be a significant
contributor to coastal erosion.

Recently the island of St. Kitts has experienced
increased demand pressures to accommodate tourism
growth.   The geographic concentration of tourism growth
on the island has been the South-East Peninsula.   In
order to preserve the environmental quality and balance
of the region, the government of St. Kitts initiated the
South-East Peninsula Land Development and Conservation
Act, 1986.   This Act was developed to provide for the
development, conservation and management of the
peninsula, through the establishment of a Land
Development and Conservation Board with specific powers
and functions:

1)   To evaluate residential, commercial, industrial
and other development schemes; and,
2)   To make recommendations concerning:
      - allotment reservation and zoning of land for
      different purposes;
      - control of pollution and maintenance of the
      environmental quality of the South-East Peninsula
      including coastal conservation;
      - development and implementation of an
      environmental protection plan; and,
      - preparation of schemes to develop lands in
      accordance with the St. Kitts/Nevis Land
      Development Control Act, 1966.

The Board also prepared a South-East Peninsula
Development and Land Use Management Plan including,
guidelines to be used in determining the suitability of
particular developmental activities in the peninsula and
specific plan elements for: Land use; Transportation
facilities; Preservation and management of the scenic
and other natural resources; recreation; waste disposal
facilities and power plants; living resources; human
settlements; agriculture and industry within the South-
East Peninsula; and, coastal conservation.   This plan
along with a Handbook of Development Guidelines and
Considerations for the South-East Peninsula was approved
by the Minister who holds the portfolio for development
in 1989.   The passage and implementation of the South-
East Peninsula Land Development and Conservation Act
effectively created a separate planning district in St.
Kitts for this peninsula.

As a follow-up to the South-East Peninsula planning
initiatives, the government of St. Kitts/Nevis adopted
a National Conservation and Environment Protection Act

(NCEPA) in 1987. This comprehensive environmental and resource management prototype was a significant step in the direction of improved coastal resource management in the country. However, comprehensive accompanying regulations are still needed to implement and enforce this act effectively. The NCEPA established however, a conservation commission that serves in an advisory capacity to the minister of the national government who holds the portfolio for development. The NCEPA also requires the formulation of national coastal zone management program no only for the South-East Peninsula, but for the entire twin island state of St. Kitts/Nevis. To date, no plans or projects have been established towards the development of a coastal zone management plan.

Both Jamaica and Trinidad and Tobago use a sectorial approach to coastal management. For instance the government of Trinidad & Tobago established an Institute of Marine Affairs in 1978 to provide basic data and information on the state of the coastal and marine environment. To date, that wealth of scientific information has not been used to develop an integrated coastal management plan for the island. Not with-standing the ongoing research interests, the Institute's expertise has been used primarily in an advisory capacity in response to coastal development proposals, problems and issues. Jamaica like Trinidad possesses a wealth of information, expertise, and technical capability to address coastal management issues. The institutional framework certainly exists to develop and implement an integrated coastal management approach. However, to date the evolution of a coordinated management process for sustainable development of Jamaica's coastal zone is still in a formative stage.

The cases cited here reflect a cross-section of the level of sophistication achieved by typical coastal management efforts in some Eastern Caribbean countries. In many circumstances coastal management activities are not institutionalized; they are reactionary and concentrate on the solution of isolated problems. As a result, coastal management in many Eastern Caribbean countries has utilized a reactive rather than proactive approach in dealing with coastal problems and issues.

Policy Considerations for Managing Land Use in the Coastal Zone

While the economies of most Eastern Caribbean nations are heavily dependent on their coastal environments, and rely extensively on this zone to sustain economic growth and development, the national physical development plans of these countries do not reflect this phenomenon. These plans are usually traditional in scope and do not target the coastal area as a specialized sector for alternative development considerations. Furthermore, these plans lack functional elements to deal specifically with the coastal area.

This apparent indifference to the coastal zone is related to the low level of governmental and public awareness of the importance of this area and its contributions to national physical development. This problem is compounded by the traditional approach to development planning which presumes that economic growth and development is always beneficial for a region or country, and the role of the planner is to organize space to accommodate this growth. Having regard to the spatial limitations of small island nations and the interrelated nature of coastal and marine ecosystems in these islands, it is not sufficient for plans to only accommodate growth demands, but in the process they must evaluate the ability of the environment to accommodate proposed growth.

The traditional planning approach in these islands has also contributed to intensive ribbon development in many coastal areas to the detriment of innovative coastal development alternatives. Barbados is a typical example of this phenomenon and the west coast of Trinidad reflects a similar trend.

The traditional planning process needs to be altered to reflect the sensitivity of the coastal zone to withstand the intensive demands of multiple use activities. Inventories must be undertaken to identify and classify coastal lands and resources. Once this data base is established, coastal lands can then be classified by use category. These categories can be used to establish major development sub-zones based on the limitations of their physical and environmental characteristics. It is important in small island nations with limited coastal land to be able to identify and assess the potential for various types of coastal development on the basis of land suitability. The application of this process will aid in the establishment of buffer zones as a controlling device for regulating coastal development.

In order to appease coastal land owners and developers
who may be affected by the establishment of these
control devices, it is suggested that Eastern Caribbean
governments consider the possibility of allowing
affected land owners to transfer their development
options to another sub-zone capable of accommodating
the type of development activity. In turn, that
vacated site could be used by another land owner with
a development proposal that fits the environmental
limitations of the area.

Although environmental impact assessments (EIA) will
add another cost factor to the planning process, it is
an essential step in the evaluation of potential coastal
development activities at the project formulation stage.
Planners must therefore be trained to interpret and
incorporate the EIA process into the appraisal of
prospective development activities.

EIAs are multi-disciplinary in nature and as such
require inputs from a broad cross-section of
disciplines and governmental agencies that have
jurisdictional responsibilities over activities and or
segments of the coastal zone. It is, therefore,
imperative that Eastern Caribbean governments in
conjunction with regional scientific organizations
and the University of the West Indies establish an
educational training program that will assist planners
and other policy makers in identifying and
incorporating coastal environmental constraints into
decision making processes and plan formulation.

Although land use controls can be effective in
regulating and influencing development in coastal sub-
zones, when these devices are used in conjunction with
tax incentives they can more effectively control the use
of coastal land. A tax classification system can be
established based on the type of coastal use activity
and the degree of environmental impacts associated with
this activity. Using environmental matrices, coastal
activities can therefore be classified based on their
propensity to pollute the marine environment, and
taxation indices can be levied based on the activity's
proclivity to pollute. Although it is difficult to
ascertain the extent of damage caused by individual
point source polluters in the coastal zone, it is also
useful to consider tax assessment as an incentive for
coastal users to utilize state of the art pollution
abatement technology.

Taxes can be levied based on the type of coastal use
and on the level of technology utilized to control

pollution elements. For example, a coastal tourism
facility that utilizes a tertiary sewage treatment
package system could be taxed at a much lower rate than
an adjacent facility that continues to use a primary
treatment system. This should be an incentive to
encourage future tourism development to incorporate
the latest technology in sewage disposal. This taxing
approach could be applied to other categories of coastal
uses.

Obstacles to Integrated Coastal Zone Management

Effective coastal zone management efforts in the
Eastern Caribbean have experienced limited success due
to the unwillingness and resistance of governmental
ministries, with jurisdictional oversight over
resources and activities within the coastal zone, to
transfer their authority to a new centralized agency.
Many ministries have also been unwilling to fully
participate in coordinated activities that would lead
to the development of an integrated management program.
These ministries and specialized agencies operate semi-
autonomously reporting directly to an elected official,
usually a minister of government holding the designated
portfolio for that ministry. Very often these
ministries become administrative sectors of competing
interests, depending on the political ambition and
direction of their cabinet minister.

A case in point could be made where a Ministry of
Tourism competes with a Ministry of Agriculture and
Fisheries for the exclusive use of a coastal resource
to the detriment of the specific coastal activity.
Numerous examples exist in the Eastern Caribbean where
coastal hotel development have displaced local
artisanal fisheries leading to a loss of access and use
of beach facilities by local fishermen. Under a
comprehensive coastal management approach, the
activities of these ministries can be coordinated in
a manner that would be beneficial to all user groups
requiring access to the waters edge for various use
activities.

Conclusion

From the issues cited previously in this paper, there
is clearly a need for Eastern Caribbean governments to
collect the types of data required by coastal area
decision makers and to reformulate this data into

information packages for legislation development, monitoring, and enforcement purposes. This process requires the establishment of a government supported coastal zone management agency with oversight authority to coordinate the many activities and regulations associated with sustainable development of the coastal area. This agency must also work in conjunction with a government appointed coastal commission comprised of representative coastal user groups, including the scientific and education community, business and manufacturing interests, including the tourism and fisheries sectors. This commission should be chaired by an elected official at the ministerial level holding the relevant portfolio. This body should be empowered to review, approve or deny coastal development proposals submitted by the coastal zone management agency.

Finally, this commission may also function as a think tank and task force to work with national disaster preparedness units to incorporate hazard mitigation measures into evolving coastal management efforts in the Eastern Caribbean. It should be noted that many researchers have cited the lack of information, training, qualified personnel, educational opportunities and inter-agency coordination problems as additional obstacles to overcome in the development of an integrated coastal management approach. However, this author believes that a major obstacle also exists in the approach to economic and physical development planning in these countries. National physical development plans must not only consider the defined coastal zone as a sub-region, but should also relinquish the traditional mind-set, that the role of planning is merely to organize physical space to accommodate growth and development activities. Planning approaches must go one step further and consider the physical and environmental limitations and impacts of proposed growth and development activities. In so doing, it is possible to accommodate the congruent objectives of coastal zone management and sustained development.

REFERENCES

Archer, A.B. 1984   "Gran Anse Beach Erosion Study. The Impact of Waste Water on Coral Reefs.   Report prepared for the OAS.

Bellairs Research Institute. 1987   "Sewage Treatment and Disposal for the Gran Anse Area of Grenada.   Report prepared for USAID and the OAS.

Cambers, G. 1983   "Coastal Erosion in St. Kitts, Nevis.   Report prepared for the Government of St. Kitts Nevis.

Cambers, G. 1987 "Coastal Zone Management Programmes in Barbados. and Grenada" Proceedings of the Fifth Symposium on Coastal and Ocean Management. American Society of Civil Engineers. Vol.2

CAMPNET Network. 1989   The Worldwide Status of CAMP - Report = 1 from Charleston.

Corker, I. R. 1988   "Nevis West Indies Zoning Map". Preliminary Report Prepared for the Land Use Office.

Jackson, I., Torres, L., John, J., Lu, S.F. 1983.   "Physical Tourism Development Plan"   Report prepared for the OAS.

Lowery, J., Barrett, A., Cambers, G. 1989.   "Nevis Coastal Monitoring Programme, Analysis of Beach Changes August 1988 to October 1989.

Lewsey, C.D. 1987   "The effects of Tourism Development on Natural Resources and Infrastructural Facilities -- The Case of Barbados" Commonwealth Science Council Publication Series, No.27.

Manwaring, G., McShine, H. 1989   "Economic Aspects of the Point Lisas Case Study".   Conference on Economics and the Environment, Barbados 1989, CCA.

Proctor & Redfern International. 1984.   "Coastal Conservation Study"   Government of Barbados.

St. Kitts/Nevis Legislation.
     The Land Development (Control) Ordinance, 1966
     The South-East Peninsula Land and Conservation Act, 1986
     The National Conservation and Environment Protection Act, 1987

Wade, B.A. 1985.   "The Impact of Increasing Pollution on Kingston Harbour, Jamaica".   Proceedings of the Caribbean Seminar on Environmental Impact Assessment, Barbados 1985.   CCA.

COASTAL LEGISLATION IN THE BRITISH VIRGIN ISLANDS

GILLIAN CAMBERS*

Abstract

The British Virgin Islands (B.V.I.), a group of fifty islands east of Puerto Rico have long been at the forefront of environmental management in the Eastern Caribbean. The B.V.I. is heavily dependent on tourism, most of which is located in the coastal zone. A major environmental workshop in 1986 recognized depletion of coastal resources as a major problem, and the need for the development of new coastal legislation was identified as a priority area. The process whereby the legislation was prepared is described, this included seven major drafts over a period of four years as well as a series of public meetings. The subject areas covered by the legislation are also described in detail, as the legislation evolved through the many drafts the focus shifted from a conservation angle to a coastal management context. During the four years a coastal management agency was set up, the Conservation and Fisheries Department and already many of the administrative procedures for implementation of the Act are in place. It is predicted that the legislation will be enacted early in 1991, regulations to the Act are being prepared. It is hoped that the legislation will provide a framework law for other islands in the region.

Introduction

The British Virgin Islands, a group of some fifty islands lying east of Puerto Rico, have long been in the forefront of environmental conservation in the Eastern Caribbean. As a result of this they are one of the first Caribbean Islands to prepare and implement coastal management legislation. This paper describes and analyses the preparation process and the legislation

*------------------
Chief Conservation & Fisheries Officer, Conservation & Fisheries Department, P.O.Box 860, Road Town, Tortola, British Virgin Islands.

itself, which although   not   perfect,   can   certainl
provide a framework for other   Caribbean Islands who ma
wish to follow a similar path in the future.

Background

The British   Virgin   Islands are a group   of   som
fifty islands, islets   and   cays   lying   150   km east o
Puerto Rico in the Lesser Antilles of the Caribbean Sea
The total land area is 153   sq   km,   the   three   larges
islands are Tortola   (54sq   km),   Anegada (38sq   km)   an
Virgin Gorda (21   sq   km),   Oldfield (1987), see Figure 1
The islands are   of   volcanic   origin   and   mountainou
except Anegada which is flat and composed of limestone.

The British   Virgin   Islands are a United   Kingdo
Dependant Territory, government   is   vested   in   th
Governor (appointed by the Crown),   an Executive Counci
and a Legislative Council.   The B.V.I. has   a populatio
of 14,500, Development Planning Unit (1988).

Tourism is   the   main   sector   of the economy wit
construction and service   industries   also   playin
important roles.   In 1987, the contribution   of   touris
to the gross   domestic   product   was   US$ 24.6   millio
representing 25.2% of G.D.P.   at   factor   cost.   Charte
yachts are the   main   sector   of   the   B.V.I.'s   touris
market, in 1989   the   proportion   of   overnight   holida
visitors using boat accomodation   was   60%,   Developmen
Planning Unit (1990).   Table   1   summarises   the   198
holiday visitor arrivals by the type of accomodation an
the type of tourism, and shows clearly that charter boa
tourists are the   most   important   group.   Cruise   shi
visitors make up the second   largest   group   in terms o
numbers of arrivals.

Table 1   Breakdown of Holiday Visitors to   the   B.V.I.i
1989
        Source : Development Planning Unit (1990).

Types of Visitors	Numbers	%
Overnight visitors staying on boats	105,841	37%
Overnight visitors staying in hotels	42,221	15%
Overnight visitors in rented/own accomodation	29,012	10%
Cruiseship visitors	71,637	25%
Excursionists	39,242	13%

FIGURE 1

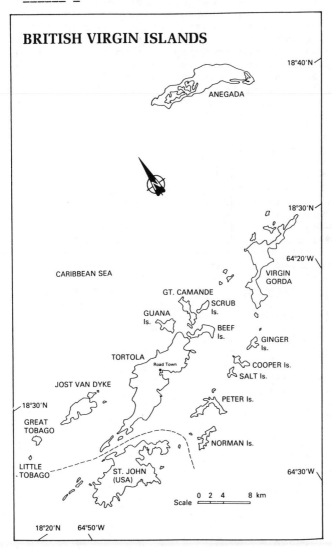

The B.V.I. has always been a leader in the field
of conservation in the Eastern Caribbean, for example,
the B.V.I National Parks Trust was established in 1961,
a detailed systems plan for conservation through parks
and protected areas has been set up and is being
implemented, B.V.I. National Parks Trust (1986).

One of the factors influencing the B.V.I.'s leadership role in environmental conservation is an understanding within the tourism industry that the natural environment is the mainstay of the industry and that visitors come to enjoy the natural environment and to enjoy cruising in its waters. The B.V.I. tourism thrust has been up-market and small scale in the past, and although this is now changing, it has helped the B.V.I. avoid much of the over-development seen in many other Caribbean Islands.

Coastal Zone Characteristics

Most of the islands are volcanic, the highest point in Tortola is 521 m. Anegada is the exception, this is a low coralline island with several major ponds and a maximum height of 8 m. Table 2 shows for the three major islands the total coastal length, the length of cliffed coast, and the length of lowland coast divided into beaches and wetlands. (In Tortola there is a third category, that of reclaimed land).

Table 2 Percentages of Lowland and Cliffed Coasts, Developed and Undeveloped Coasts in the Three Largest Islands of the B.V.I.
Source : Cambers (1990).

	Tortola km	Tortola %	Virgin Gorda km	Virgin Gorda %	Anegada km	Anegada %
Total coastal length	78	100	58	100	42	100
Length of cliff coast	44	56	40.5	70	0	0
Beach length	16.0	21	13.5	23	32	76
Length of wetland coast	11.0	14	4.0	7	10	24
Length of reclaimed coast	7.0	9	0	0	0	0
Total beach length	16.0	100	13.5	100	32	100
Developed beach length	8	50	3.4	25	1.6	5
Total wetland length	11.0	100	4.0	100	10.0	100
Developed wetland	5.5	50	0.4	10	0.5	5

Table 2 also shows the percentage of lowland coast that
has development located immediately   behind   it.   The
table shows that   Tortola is the most developed island,
50% of the beaches have development immediately behind
them as do 50 % of the wetlands.   Virgin Gorda has a
lower percentage of lowland coast and that is less
developed than in Tortola. While in Anegada, the entire
coast is classified as a lowland coast and 90% of that
is undeveloped.

        The B.V.I. has extensive   nearshore reef systems,
based on the topographic survey maps there is a total
area of 107 sq km of coral reefs. The Horseshoe Reef
system which extends south of Anegada is the largest
reef system in the Lesser Antilles, Oldfield (1987).

Coastal Zone Management Prior to 1986

        Prior to 1986 there were only small piecemeal
attempts to manage the coastal zone.   The main focus was
on conservation rather than management.   The post of
Conservation Officer was established within the Ministry
of Natural Resources & Labour, however, the main thrust
was to work with the National Parks Trust on the
preparation and implementation   of   the   Parks   and
Protected Areas Systems Plan.

        With so little flat land in most of the islands
the emphasis and pressure on the coastal zone is
considerable. In addition the main focus of the economy
is on tourism almost all of which is located in the
coastal zone. As a result of these two factors and the
increased rate of the Territory's development seen in
the 1980's, coastal resources were rapidly becoming
depleted. This was manifest in the widespread beach
erosion resulting from beach sand mining (beach sand is
used for construction), the filling in of salt ponds,
the reclamation of land and loss of mangroves, the
pollution with solid and liquid waste of the coastal
zone, badly planned development in the coastal zone, the
loss of coral reefs and seagrass beds through boat
anchoring, the reduction of nearshore fish stocks, etc.

        Depletion of coastal resources was recognized to
be a major problem and a four day workshop was held on
this subject sponsored by the Organisation of Eastern
Caribbean States Natural Resources Management Unit
(OECS-NRMU), (1986). The major goals identified in this
workshop were :

   (1) To control beach sand mining;

(2)   To preserve selected mangrove areas;
(3)   To enforce existing legislation;
(4)   To establish performance controls;
(5)   To control pollution.

In 1986 the Government of the B.V.I. requested technical legal assistance from the OECS-NRMU to strengthen and update existing environmental legislation. The priority area was coastal conservation legislation.

The Preparation of Coastal Legislation 1987-1991

Following this request by the B.V.I Government for technical assistance, a broad outline for coastal conservation legislation was developed by Lausche (1987). After consultation with Government it was decided that the key elements to be included in the law should be as follows :

(1)   Overall administration to be with the Ministry of Natural Resources and Labour, and daily administration to be with a conservation office (to be set up);
(2)   Coastal setbacks to be clearly defined, 75-100 feet from the foreshore with a public right of way 6 feet from the foreshore;
(3)   To reaffirm the foreshore is vested in the Crown, and to redefine the foreshore as extending to the vegetation line;
(4)   To have at least one public access to each beach;
(5)   To develop a coastal plan for the B.V.I. to show special use areas, conservation areas, foreshore, setbacks etc.
(6)   To restrict cruise ship anchorages to certain areas and to collect fees;
(7)   To protect ghauts (streams) and watersheds;
(8)   To require environmental impact assessments for major development projects;
(9)   To make regulations in matters relating to coastal conservation.

These were the key elements included in the first draft in 1987. After the Consultant finished work in 1987, the draft was then reworked by the Parliamentary Counsel in the Attorney General's Office in consultation with the Conservation Officer in 1988.

In February 1988 a regional workshop on environmental legislation was organised by the OECS-NRMU and held in the B.V.I.

In December, 1988, the draft coast conservation bill was circulated to other Government Departments for comments. The Coast Conservation Bill had the first reading in Legislative Council in August 1989, the recommendation was that the bill should be made available to the public and discussed at a series of public meetings.

Following this decision, a series of some fourteen public meetings were scheduled and held between October and December 1989 at the following centres :

- Tortola   : Road Town, Sea Cows Bay, Frenchmans Cay, Cappoons Bay, Carrot Bay, Cane Garden Bay, Brewers Bay, Long Look, East End, Baughers Bay;
- Virgin Gorda : The Valley, North Sound/Gun Creek;
- Anegada   : The Settlement;
- Jost van Dyke: Great Harbour.

At each meeting the bill was distributed to the attendees and the main elements of the bill were described, following which there was discussion. The meetings were recorded on tape cassettes as well as in writing. Some of the meetings were well attended with as many as 50 persons, others were poorly attended. The discussions were usually very specific to the particular area, for instance persons in the Long Look area were most concerned about beach sand mining at Josiahs Bay while persons at Frenchmans Cay were most concerned about the loss of the mangroves and the effects on fishing.

Meetings were also held with special interest groups such as the Hotel and Commerce Association. Several persons and groups also sent in written comments on the bill. The meetings were completed in March 1990.

Following the public meetings, the comments were summarised and the bill was revised in the light of these comments. Not all the comments were incorporated into the revised bill, however, they do remain on file and therefore on record. Most of this work was done by the Conservation Office in consultation with the Ministry of Natural Resources and Labour. (The Conservation Office was set up in January 1989).

Following this revision, the bill was then redrafted by the Parliamentary Counsel of the Attorney General's Office, such that the final bill was ready for presentation to the Legislative Council in January 1991. The bill had by this time been renamed the Coast Conservation and Management Bill and had been through seven drafts.

The Coast Conservation & Management Act of 1991

          The bill is described as follows :
"An Act to provide for the conservation, management, and
development of the coastal lands and waters of the
Virgin Islands; to regulate and control development
activities within the coastal zone; and to provide for
matters connected therewith or incidental thereto".

          The bill ensures that no development should take
place in the coastal zone without a coastal zone permit.
The coastal zone starts 100 yards landward of the spring
high water mark and extends to the outer limit of the
territorial sea (3 nautical miles from the shoreline of
the Territory). Figure 2 shows the coastal zone is
divided into three segments :

    1. The adjoining land - spring high water mark to 100
       yards inland on a lowland coast, or where there is
       a cliff 50 feet inland from the cliff edge;
    2. The beach - the seaward line of the foreshore to
       the vegetation line or other natural barrier, the
       foreshore lies between mean low water mark and mean
       high water mark;
    3. The coastal waters - the sea, and those waters
       adjacent to the landward line of the adjoining land
       or connected permanently or intermittently with the
       sea.

          Development activity is defined comprehensively to
include all activities such as building on land or in
the sea, additions, renovations and removals, filling
and reclamation, discharge of any solid or liquid waste,
dredging, mining, subdivision, removal of any natural
vegetation, including mangroves, land clearance for
agriculture and the removal or harvesting of coral.

          Thus for any development activity a coastal permit
is required. Conditions are set out for coastal zone
permit application such that an applicant may apply for
provisional approval first and then final approval,
however, provisional approval would not allow the
applicant to start the activity. An applicant may apply
for full approval in the first instance. Major projects
require an environmental impact assessment report, the
requirements for such a report are listed. A provision
is also included whereby the public have to be informed
of applications for major development activities by
notice published in the Gazette, and provision made for
the public to review the applications and comment.

FIGURE 2   THE   COASTAL   ZONE   AS   DEFINED   IN   THE   COAST
CONSERVATION & MANAGEMENT ACT OF 1991.

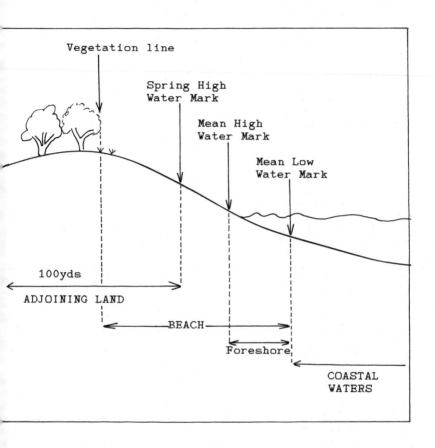

The Act is to be administered by the Minister of
Natural Resources and Labour. One of the most important
and universal conclusions from the public meetings was
that this act placed too much responsibility on one
person, the Minister.   As a result the final Act was
amended such that a Coast Conservation and Management
Advisory Commitee is to be set up to assist the Minister
in reviewing all applications for development and other
matters to do with the coastal zone. This is to be a
multi-disciplinary committee and to include representatives from the following Government departments :

    Conservation and Fisheries Department,
    Survey Department,

Town and Country Planning Department,
Ports Authority,
Ministry of Natural Resources & Labour,
Public Health Department,

as well as up to five representatives from the public.

The Act vests the foreshore in the Crown, this had
previously been applied from British law, however, this
Act reaffirms the ownership of the foreshore. It should
be noted that the initial outline produced by Lausche
(1987) had recommended that the foreshore be extended to
the vegetation line, however, this proved not to be
practical in the B.V.I. where much of the land from the
mean high water mark to the vegetation line is in
private ownership.

The Act also provides for there to be at least one
public landward access to each beach in the Territory.
Provision is made for establishing public accesses
through traditional public use, gift, negotiation,
exchange for other property and compulsory acquisition.

Provision is made within the Act for Special
Resource Areas whereby resources such as mangroves, sea
grass beds, coral reefs etc. may be protected from
destruction or deterioration. In addition, Special Use
Areas may be declared under the Act where public use of
certain lands and waters needs to be controlled eg.
protected swimming and surfing areas where other
conflicting uses are prohibited.

Beach sand mining has long been a problem in the
B.V.I., this Act states that there shall be no sand
mining from the foreshore or any part of the coastal
zone without a coastal permit. (There have been many
problems in the past with interpretation of the Beach
Protection Ordinance). In addition a coastal permit is
required for the transport of sand, gravel and other
mineral resources from the coastal zone and the Act
gives an authorised officer the right to stop any
vehicle, vessel or other craft to ascertain whether a
permit has been issued.

Pollution of the coastal zone with oil, sewage,
solid or liquid waste or other waste is prohibited
within this Act.

The Act imposes various penalties up to US$ 20,000
for contravention of its clauses. Where development
activities have been conducted without coastal zone
permits, or where conditions of permits have been
contravened, a cease and desist order may be issued.

Following conviction, if the particular activity is continued, a daily fine of US$ 1,000 may be imposed. Another important provision allows for the Court to order restoration, rehabilitation or clean up of the affected area. Should such a restoration order not be complied with the work could be carried out by Government and recovered as a civil debt.

Finally the Act is binding on the Crown, this is a very important clause since often Government Agencies are major offenders when it comes to environmental conservation legislation.

When the final Act is compared with the broad outline developed by Lausche (1987), it can be seen that most of the major provisions have been included. As previously stated the limits of the foreshore were not expanded because of the private ownership issue. The area from the mean high water mark to the vegetation line remains in private ownership in most areas without any clear definition of the public's right to use this area. In this respect the B.V.I. is similar to most other Eastern Caribbean countries. Coastal setbacks will be clearly defined in the regulations to the Act. Control of cruise ship anchorages can be accomodated under the special use and special resource areas. However, the provision in the Lausche (1987) outline to protect ghauts and watersheds has not been included in this Act.

In the early drafts the Act was perceived mainly as a conservation act, however, as it evolved through several drafts and several years work, the management aspect became clearer and more important, such that the title was changed from the Coast Conservation bill to the Coast Conservation and Management bill. This is important in that it reflects a growing realisation in the B.V.I. that the conservation versus development controversy can be resolved through effective coastal zone management such that the goal of sustainable development becomes a reality.

Coastal Zone Management Since 1986

In 1986 the depletion of coastal resources was recognized by the Government to be a major problem and one of the solutions was to draw up new legislation. However, this was not the only solution and things did not stand still while the new legislation was being prepared. Instead several important management steps were implemented between 1986 and 1991.

In 1988 it was decided to set up a Conservation Office, and this became a reality in January 1989 when the Conservation Office was set up as a technical unit under the Ministry of Natural Resources & Labour. In 1990 the Conservation Office was merged with the Fisheries Division to become a Conservation & Fisheries Department (CFD).

The major functions of the CFD are as follows :

- application review and environmental planning,
- environmental monitoring,
- fisheries management,
- environmental awareness and education,
- surveillance, enforcement and legislation.

Already some administrative procedures relating to the future Coast Conservation & Management Act (CCMA) have been implemented. Applications for specific developments (moorings, jetties, reclamations, sand mining) in the coastal zone are reviewed by an inter-agency committee, which is a prototype for the Coastal Conservation and Management Advisory Committee defined under the CCMA. This committee was set up in 1989, and in 1990 eleven meetings were held and 56 applications reviewed.

Environmental monitoring programmes are in place for water quality, beach changes, turtle populations, mangrove resources. Surveillance of all permitted coastal development is conducted although in many cases the actual enforcement has to await the enactment of the CCMA. A very important part of the Department's work is public awareness at all levels of the community – schools, public, politicians, special interest groups. Thus a coastal zone management programme is evolving in the B.V.I., an important start has been made since 1986, but it is recognized that there is still a long way to go, particularly in relation to development planning/ zoning of the coastal zone.

Implementation of the Coast Conservation & Management Act

It is foreseen that the Act will be passed early in 1991. One of the most important aspects is public awareness and acceptance of the Act. Although several public meetings were held in 1989/90, it is estimated that less than 5% of the population attended the meetings. Thus there is a need to highlight certain sections of the Act for the public. To this end a programme has been drawn up such that the press and

radio will be used to bring different sections of the
Act to the public's attention during the rest of 1991.

In addition workshops are being planned with
enforcement officers, in particular the police, to
emphasise certain aspects of the Act and how to enforce
them.

Technical assistance has been obtained from the
OECS-NRMU to prepare regulations for the CCMA. A first
draft of the regulations were prepared in 1990 and a
second draft is in preparation. It is envisaged that
the regulations for the Act should be in place by 1992.
Administrative procedures and handbooks are also being
developed as part of this technical assistance.

Conclusions and Recommendations

The CCMA has been many years in the making, four
and a half years from conception to a final version, and
seven major drafts. The preparation of new legislation
is usually a very time consuming process in the Eastern
Caribbean Islands, and the B.V.I. is certainly no
exception. The time and work involved is considerable,
especially when new ground is being broken, as was the
case with this environmental legislation for there were
no proven regional models.

During the process of preparation of the CCMA, new
administrative agencies and procedures had to be
established and this also added to the time factor.
Nevertheless the B.V.I. is now in the position where it
has a Coastal Zone Management Agency and appropriate
legislation to manage the coastal zone. This in indeed
a major step forward and it is hoped that the B.V.I. can
use these tools to become a model for the region.

However, the B.V.I. realises that the major
challenge lies ahead in the implementation of the CCMA.
It is hoped that the CCMA can be used as a framework law
for the region and the B.V.I. experience with coastal
legislation and its implementation can be used as a
model for the region.

****

References

Cambers, G. 1989. The impact and response to sea level
rise in the islands of the Eastern Caribbean.
Unpublished report prepared for the Environmental

Protection Agency.

Development Planning Unit. 1990. British Virgin Islands Social and Economic Review 1988.

Lausche, B. 1987. Harmonisation of environmental legislation. 3 BVI. Organisation of Eastern Caribbean States - Natural Resources Management Project Activity.

National Parks Trust & Eastern Caribbean Natural Area Management Program. 1986. A parks and protected areas system plan for the British Virgin Islands.

OECS-Natural Resources Management Unit. 1986. Management of Coastal Resources in BVI. 2 BVI.

Oldfield, S. 1987. Fragments of Paradise. Pisces Publications.

****

PROBLEMS OF COASTAL ZONE MANAGEMENT IN ANTIGUA AND BARBUDA

by

David Freestone *

ABSTRACT

The number of beaches and the beauty of the coastal areas of Antigua and Barbuda have been the basis for a steep rise in tourism in the last decade, which has resulted in a commensurate acceleration of development in the coastal zone. The building of hotel and tourism related facilities has resulted in the draining of important saltpond and mangrove areas, and the need for deep water access for cruise ships has necessitated the dredging of harbour areas. Such developments threaten possible long term environmental damage. Because of the priority which has been given to the development of tourism and its wealth generating importance, it is only recently that attention has started to be given to the co-ordination of the activities which put considerable stress on the coastal zone, and to the establishment of institutions which would permit an informed and long term view of the future development of the coastal zone. This paper assesses the legislative and institutional responses to these problems.

* Institute of Estuarine and Coastal Studies, and Senior Lecturer in Law, University of Hull, England. Managing Editor, **International Journal of Estuarine and Coastal Law,** Graham and Trotman/Martinus Nijhoff, London/Dordrecht. From January 1987 to December 1988, Adviser, Ministry of Foreign Affairs, Antigua and Barbuda.

The author is most grateful to Oscar Bird, Chairman of the Historical, Conservation and Environment Commission and Colin Murdoch, Senior Foreign Service Officer, Antigua and Barbuda for their comments on a previous draft of this paper. The final text is however his sole responsibility.

The "twin island" state of Antigua and Barbuda is situated in the Lesser Antilles in the Eastern Caribbean. It is distinguished even in the Caribbean for the number of its beaches, and the beauty of its coastal areas. These natural assets have been the basis for a steep rise in tourism in the last decade, which has resulted in a commensurate acceleration of development in the coastal zone. As a result, although Barbuda remains largely undeveloped, the coastal zone of Antigua is the single area most important to the economy of the state. It is also the area under the most stress, for there appears to be little co-ordinated and effective management of conflicting uses. The unprecedented boom in waterside building and development projects, increased usage from watersports and yachting, as well as sport and commercial fishing. The coastal zone is also being used for waste disposal.

Direct and Indirect tourism income is estimated currently to provide more than 60% of Antigua/Barbuda's GNP. A growing number of visitors a year are concentrated in (predominantly beach front) hotels and condominions and there are substantial further arrivals by cruise ship. Hotel and tourism development is predominantly funded by external/foreign investors, although the Government has recently funded a number of major developments including the prestigious Royal Antiguan Hotel and Heritage Quay, a casino and shopping complex aimed at the cruiseship market on the waterfront in St John's - the islands' capital city. Both these developments have required extensive dredging operations. The former to transform a saltpond into a marina area and the latter to allow cruise ships to anchor alongside the waterfront. Disposal of dredge spoil has been a problem for both projects.

Hotel capacity is still expanding and projects under construction could double the number of beds available in the next five years. These sites are virtually all beachfront and adjacent properties in to-date underdeveloped areas of the island. A number of sites under development have resulted in largescale destruction of or major damage to mangrove swamps (eg at Jolly Beach, the Flashes, Nonesuch Bay) and salt ponds (eg Deep Bay, Jolly Beach and Mackinnons) which are important fish breeding areas and wild life habitats. It is also established that mangrove destruction prevents filtering of runoff water allowing sediments to choke reef systems. There is evidence of such reef damage in a number of areas - which relates not only to mangrove destruction but also to the fact that for a relatively flat island Antigua has a very high incidence of soil erosion. Lack of sewage infrastructure in St John's and inadequate or inadequately maintained sewage and waste disposal systems in other areas (notably from hotels) must also have contributed to such damage. (Jackson, 1986) Of course, on a small island virtually all land-based pollution ends up in the sea.

As a part of a general coastal management plan, the following areas could be identified as in particular need of action:

1. Regulation of Leisure/Tourist Uses of the Coast:

Safety regulations for watersports
Although some hotels have defacto established safety regimes for watersports, and legislation already regulates certain activities (eg the 1976 Beach Control (Prevention of Danger) Regulations, SRO No. 25 of 1976) this is not rigorously enforced. Uniform and enforced national safety standards are overdue.

2. Designation and enforcement of primary use regimes and or protected areas for certain marine areas, eg designated recreational areas for water sports, scuba diving, glass bottomed boats, etc,to prevent conflicts with local fishermen. Enforcement of existing protected areas, prohibition on the taking of coral, use of spear fishing (either generally or within certain areas)

3. Active Protection of important Coastal Areas.
Designation of certain mangrove areas, wetlands and seagrass areas for preservation.:
It has been clearly established that these areas are vital as fish breeding areas essential to the well being of fishstocks over a wide area, they also filter sediments from run-off water preventing siltation on beach and reef areas.

Migrant and resident birds also use these areas. Unusual and diverse bird stocks are an important natural asset, hence their habitat needs attention and preservation.

4. Control of Land based Pollution
A complete prohibition on waste and sewage discharges into coastal waters or into surface water which will find its way into the sea is required. The marine ecosystems of coral reef areas have a very low tolerance to pollution. The reefs of Antigua/Barbuda protect the beaches from heavy

tides and provide a vital resource for fishing and tourism. Damage is already widely reported on inshore reef areas.

5. Sea Borne Pollution

A major oil slick on the beaches of Antigua could have a potentially disastrous effect on the economy. An oil spill contingency plan has been drawn up and tested. Antigua/Barbuda is in the process of becoming a party to the International Oil Pollution Conventions, which provide proper compensation from insurance and in default from internationally established funds.(eg 1969 International Convention on civil liability for oil pollution damage and the 1971 International Convention on the establishment of an international fund for compensation for oil pollution damage, it has decided to defer consideration of accession to the1984amendments to these regimes) Antigua/Barbuda is a party to MARPOL 1973/78, but the international Conventions will require a clearer legislative foundation in national law.

6. Building Regulations

A number of building practices have contributed to environmental damage to the coast. Buildings too close to the water's edge, widespread clearing of all vegetation on beach areas, construction of groynes and solid jetties, have all contributed to erosion of beaches. In heavily developed areas such practices could result in the total loss of the beach and traditional fishing areas, as has happened in other areas of the Caribbean.

Existing Coastal and Marine Environmental Protection legislation.

A number of acts create powers to designate protected areas and to enact detailed anti-pollution regulations. In the past the problem has been with the lack of manpower, and it must be said political will, to seriously address these issues. That political climate is now changing and there are now signs of recognition at the highest levels of the seriousness of the possible results of environmental degradation. (see eg, 1989 Speech of Welcome to the 15th OECS Authority Meeting, by Deputy Prime Minister Lester Bird).

A body of legislation (some of it dating from the colonial era) is still in force regulating the resources of the coastal zone. Noteworthy are the 1957 Beach

Protection Ordinance (cap 298 of 1957) and the 1959 Beach Control Ordinance (cap 297 of 1957) . Section 4(1) of the 1957 Ordinance makes it a criminal offence for any person to:

> "(a) dig, take or carry away, or aid or assist in digging, taking or carrying away for building or construction purposes or for the purpose of providing ballast for vessels any sand, shingle or gravel from any beach or seashore in the Colony; or
>
> (b) convey or move for building or construction purposes or for the purpose of providing ballast for vessels any such sand shingle or gravel along any public road, except under and in accordance with a written permit from the Director of Public works or an authosized officer and subject to such terms and conditions therein stipulated."

Erosion caused by excavation of building materials on beaches has been a problem in Antigua, as it is everywhere in the Caribbean. Standard practice had been that PWD identified suitable sites and did the mining for sale to the public. Lausche (1986) reports that the practice has been discontinued in Antigua because of concern for the beaches, yet evidence on the ground suggests that this is an excessively sanguine view. Sand mining does go on although its status is not always clear. Certainly many major projects requiring such materials are often government sponsored. The act does not apply to Barbuda where an Antigua-based sand mining operation takes sand with the permission of the local council, but without, it appears, scientific environmental monitoring. There are reports of increasing local opposition to beach sand mining, but inland resources also exist.

The Beach Control Ordinance vests all rights in and over the foreshore and the 'floor of the sea' in the Crown and confers on the Minister [of Agriculture, Fisheries and Lands] the right to regulate the use of this area and adjoining land to a distance of "not more than fifty yards beyond the landward limit of the foreshore" and to licence its use

> "for any public purpose, or for, or in connection with, any trade, business or commercial enterprise to any person, upon such conditions and in such form as he may think fit." (section 5(1)).

In considering applications for such licences the Minister must consider

"... what public interests in regard to fishing, bathing or recreation or in regard to any future development of the land adjoining that part of the foreshore in respect of which the application is made, require to be protected, and he may provide for the protection of such interests by and in the terms of the licence or otherwise..." (section 5(3))

It is unclear to what extent these important powers are co-ordinated with the general planning process established by the 1977 Land Development and Control Act which until 1990 was administered by a different Ministry - that of Labour and Housing -until Housing was separated from the Labour Ministry. Nor is it always clear whether major development projects often directly authorised by Cabinet fit within that planning process.

Recent legislation has conferred extensive regulatory powers on government to meet general environmental risks and coastal management concerns. Although the legislative powers available are in themselves adequate, an overview demonstrates the need for a coordinated approach to environmental matters in general and to coastal zone management in particular. Not only are the legislative powers distributed among a number of acts, they also confer regulatory powers on a number of different Ministries.

The following acts give powers to various Ministers [in brackets]:

    1972 Marine Areas Act, [Minister of Agriculture]

    1983 Fisheries Act [Minister of Agriculture]

    1984 National Parks Act [Minister of Tourism]

    1985 Merchant Shipping Act [Minister of Labour]

    1986 Maritime Areas Act [Minister of Foreign Affairs]

However only one set of implementing regulations designating protected areas have yet been passed (under the 1972 Act). These designate two marine protected areas: Dimond [sic] and Salt Fish Tail Reefs in Antigua and Palaster Reef in Barbuda, (The Marine Areas (Preservation and Enhancement) Regulations, SRO No. 25, 1973, and the Marine Areas (Restricted Areas) Order, SRO No. 47, 1973). These are not systematically enforced.

The National Parks Act specifically designates historic Nelson's Dockyard a National Park and the implementation of the legislation - which does not receive direct financial support from the government - designates a wider geographical area for the national park stretching from Mamora Bay to Rendezvous Bay including adjacent marine areas. No specific protection measures have yet been suggested for these marine areas which include a few important reefs systems. Cabinet has also designated a number of areas as priority for protection, but to date action has only been taken on one - Half Moon Bay - close to the exclusive Mill Reef Club - which is funded by private sources.

Institutional Responses

As will be evident from the preceding discussion, environmental concerns are the most pressing aspects of coastal management in Antigua and Barbuda. Until the 1980s environmental concerns were perceived largely in terms of pollution and waste management both of which came under the jurisdiction of the Ministry of Health. However the escalation of interest in the environment worldwide has led to a wider view of the legitimate concerns of Government with the environment. Many of the wide range of matters within this wider environmental spectrum are spread over several Ministries and institutions.

For some years there has been within the Ministry of Economic Development, Tourism and Energy (one of the countries most significant Ministries, headed by the Deputy Prime Minister) the post of Conservation Officer, but the role of this officer was seen in relation to historic monuments - indeed until his death in 1988 the last incumbent was also Chairman of the Historic Sites Commission. The increased awareness of environmental issues in the country, manifested by the formation of an environmental NGO - and pressure, partly from regional and international agencies led to the establishment by Cabinet of a new body, to replace the Historic Sites Commission, to be called the Historical, Conservation and Environmental Commission and also to the establishment of an Environmental Desk in the Ministry of Economic Development. It is planned that the post of Conservation Officer should be re-instituted and that a Secretary to the Commission be appointed.

This does not amount to the creation of an Environment portfolio alongside the other subjects covered by the Ministry of Economic Development since a number of 'environmental services' still fall under different

Ministries. The Historical, Conservation and
Environmental Commission (HCEC) however serves as a
meeting point for senior representatives of those
Ministries and other statutory bodies such as the
Development Control Authority, the National Parks
Authority and the Port Authority together with
representatives of two NGOs - the Environmental
Awareness Group and the Archeological and Historical
Society. A private citizen interested in wildlife
protection is also a member. There is as yet no
statutory basis for this Commission. It is chaired by a
former Permanent Secretary of the Ministry of Health,
Education and Social Services. Initially, the Commission
has been concerned with holding a watching brief on
environmental matters but the Commission itself drew up
and presented proposals to Cabinet for formal terms of
reference - which included powers of intervention. After
some delay these were approved by Cabinet in November
1990.

Conclusions

There is within the Caribbean as within the rest of the
world, a growing recognition of the need to halt and
remedy environmental damage, and to ensure that economic
developmetns are sustainable within the terms of the
Bruntland Report (1988). A number of important
developments at sub-regional and regional levels support
these ideas. Antigua/Barbuda participates in the UNEP
Caribbean Environment Programme, is aparty to the
Cartagena Convention for the protection and development
of the marine environment of the Wider Caribbean, and
after playing an active role in the negotiations was the
first signatory of the 1990 Kingston Protocol to that
Convention on Specially Protected Areas and Wildlife
(Freestone, 1990). The Country is also a member of both
the Caribbean Community (CARICOM) and the Organisation
of Eastern Caribbean States (OECS). In 1989, the CARICOM
Environment Ministers issued from their Post of Spain
Meeting an important Accord on the Management and
Conservation of the Caribbean Environment (Port of Spain
Accord, 1989). The OECS Natural Resources Management
Unit, based in St Lucia, already involved in a number of
subregional prjects, is proposing the establishment of
national advisory committees on natural resource issues.
The Barbados based Caribbean Conservation Association is
also providing important impetus for national
environmental.protection initiatives, including country
studies.

The experience of Antigua and Barbuda is not untypical
in the Eastern Caribbean region. The concerted drive to

attract tourism for economic development has brought with it many unforeseen and unlooked for consequences - foremost among which is environmental damage to the coastal zone. Coastal Zone Management has not been seen as a priority by Government and hence the legislative powers available do not provide a coherent framework. Existing legislation probably provides all the necessary powers, but a new. overarching legislative framework - similar perhaps to the coastal zone management act in the British Virgin Islands - might well provide a vehicle for coordinated action as well as demonstrate a political commitment to environmental protection. Although institutions are now being put into place, a legislative foundation might also identify a clearer institutional framework within which donor agencies could more effectively channel assistance to this important area.

REFERENCES

Hon Lester Bird, Deputy Prime Minister of Antigua and Barbuda, Speech of Welcome made on behalf of the Government of Antigua and Barbuda at the Opening of the Fifteenth Meeting of the Authority of the Organisation of Eastern Caribbean States, held in Antigua, June 1-2, 1989.

CARICOM Environment Ministers, 'Port of Spain Accord on the Managment and Conservation of the Caribbean Environment.' Reproduced in (1990) 5 **International Journal of Estuarine and Coastal Law** 398-400.

David Freestone, 'Specially Protected Areas and Wildlife in the Caribbean: the 1990 Kingston Protocol to the Cartagena Convention' (1990) 5 **International Journal of Estuarine and Coastal Law** 362-382.

Ivor Jackson, 'Tourism and Environment Case Study of Fort James- Dickensen Bay, Antigua', May 1986, ECLAC.

Barbara Lausche, 'Country Report on National Legislation Relating to Natural Resource Management: Antigua and Barbuda', September 1986, OECS Natural Resources Management Project (in co-operation with OAS and GTZ).

THE PERCEIVED EFFECTIVENESS OF COASTAL WARNING SIGNS

A T WILLIAMS[1] & M J WILLIAMS[1]

Abstract

Fifteen hazard warning signs, including two currently used on beaches/cliffs at the Glamorgan Heritage Coast, Wales, UK, were tested via a semantic differential test. Results showed that signs incorporating both pictorial and written information were most effective in presenting the hazard of dangerous cliffs. Current signs on the GHC are word only signs.

Introduction

The failure of current coastal rockfall hazard warning signs to prompt changes in user behaviour to a satisfactory degree suggests that signs, despite being seen by large numbers of users (Williams & Williams 1988) are either inadequate as a persausive medium or ineffective because of poor design. The design characteristics of signs currently sited at the Glamorgan Heritage Coast,(GHC), Wales, UK were considered. In some aspects they were found to be at variance with design recommendations made by the Countryside Commission (1981); in particular, the failure to use pictorial images (symbols) to convey the warning. Empirical evidence (Szlichicinski, 1979) has suggested that symbolic signs are often a useful and attractive way of conveying messages and in some instances can perform better than worded signs. This has particularly been noted when viewing conditions have been restricted, when travelling on highways at speed or in poor weather conditions (Ells & Dewar, 1979).

----

1. Coastal Research Unit, Science and Chemical Engineering Department, Polytechnic of Wales, Pontypridd, Mid Glamorgan, South Wales, UK, CF37 1OZ.

Experiment

The aim was to determine the perceived effectiveness of current signs and to find out if the use of pictorial images would increase the potential value of signs as a rockfall hazard adjustment. A semantic differential test was employed to determine the effectiveness of fifteen hazard warning signs. The test is a "simple and inexpensive paper and pencil test ..." (Dewar & "Ells, 1977; 183), developed by Osgood et al. (1957) to measure the degree of psychological meaning of places, concepts and objects. The method is described as:

> "We provide the subject with a concept to be differentiated and a set of bi-poplar adjectives against which to do it, his only task being to indicate, for each time (pairing of a concept to a scale), the direction of this association and its intensity on a seven step scale."

> (Osgood et al. 1957;20)

For example, a subject rating stimuli (in this paper, rockfall warning signs) on the bi-polar adjective scale good-bad who believed a sign was effective in conveying its message would indicate a strong level of association towards the adjective good. Conversely, a subject believing the sign to be of poor design would do the opposite (Table 1).

The Stimuli

The stimuli presented for the subjects to rate were fifteen rockfall hazard warning signs (Plates 1-15). The signs were constructed to scale using 'Letraset' products and measured approximately 10 x 15 cms. The signs were then photographed to produce a series of symbolic images and words of varying arrangements. Two signs currently sited at the GHC (Plates 2 and 11) were included in the fifteen in order to compare their performance against new experimental designs.

The new signs were designed to be educational, incorporating such images as birds dislodging blocks/blocks shattering on the wave-cut platform (Plate 5).

Care was taken to avoid 'alarmist' designs, as management do not desire a reduction in the use of the coast through fear. Heritage Coast philosophy aims to facilitate both conservation <u>and public</u>

```
        Good1_;__;__;__;__;__;_;7Bad           E
        Weak7_;__;__;__;__;__;_;1Strong         P
      Active1_;__;__;__;__;__;_;7Passive        A
Unpredictable7_;__;__;__;__;__;_;1Predictable   U
       Clean1_;__;__;__;__;__;_;7Dirty          E
        Slow7_;__;__;__;__;__;_;1Fast           A
   Worthless7_;__;__;__;__;__;_;1Valuable       E
      Rugged1_;__;__;__;__;__;_;7Delicate       P
     Strange7_;__;__;__;__;__;_;1Familiar       U
      Simple1_;__;__;__;__;__;_;7Complicated    U
       Light7_;__;__;__;__;__;_;1Heavy          P
       Sharp1_;__;__;__;__;__;_;7Dull           A
```

                                          FACTOR

The polarity of adjective pairs is shown to indicate the
procedure for scoring.   A low score indicates a high
degree of meaning.   This information was not indicated
on the answer sheets used by participating subjects.

Stimuli are rated on four factors, with three adjective
pairs relating to each factor as indicated.   The factors
are given below with subjective meanings.

(E)   Evaluative - Attitude, Opinion of.
(U)   Understandability - Comprehension, Understanding
(P)   Potency - Strength, Power
(A)   Activity - Energy, Action

Table 1   Semantic Differential Scale (after, Dewar &
Ells, 1977)

usage for the benefit of local economies (Williams, 1987). Several of Easterby's (1977) pictogram design principles were considered relevant, ie, symbols should:

i.   Have a solid boundary - to create contrast and attract attention.

ii.   Be simple - in order for ease of perception.

iii.   Be stable - to avoid images becoming ambiguous: eg, Ruben's face/vase silhouette profiles.

Only 3 colours were used in sign construction - white, red and black. This is consistent with current hazard warning signs on UK highways (Plate 10) and at the GHC. Experimentation with colour, and also shape and movement, was considered to be too complex in what was essentially a limited study. It is recognised, however, that research regarding these aspects of design would be useful.

In order to determine whether symbols were best used alone, or in conjunction with words, 5 sign pairings were established: Plates 4/12, 6/1, 7/8, 13/3 and 15/10. The later sign of each pairing was of identical design to that of its partner apart from the inclusion of a worded message. This allowed a comparison to be made between the two techniques.

Administration

Thirty subjects drawn from the undergraduate population at the Polytechnic of Wales took part in the experiment. The subjects were collectively shown the series of 15 slides in random order, following a short talk as to the nature of the hazard and where the signs were likely to appear. On first showing each slide was viewed for 10 seconds. This was done in order for the subjects to familiarise themselves with the fifteen signs and to avoid position order effects: that is, the overrating of the first or last few signs. On second showing the same order was used, but each slide was now projected for one minute. During this time each subject completed a semantic differential test (Table 1); fifteen in total. No collusion between subjects was permitted while the exercise was in progress.

Results

Semantic differential scores were calculated for each

sign using a one to seven scale (Table 1). Scores were given for each of the four factors, with the lowest indicating the most positive evaluation. This was achieved by determining mean scores for the adjective pairs relevant to each factor. Results are presented in Table 2, along with an overall-index rating calculated by adding the four factor scores and determing the mean. This allowed each sign to be given a position ranking of between 1 and 15. Plate 8 proved to be the most positively rated sign, above two signs currently sited at the coast (Plates 2 and 11), which ranked 3rd and 11th respectively (Plates 2 and 11).

A comparison of the size sign scores - Plates 4/12, 6/1, 7/8, 13/3 and 15/10 (Table 3) - showed that in almost every instance the use of worded messages in conjunction with symbols improved the semantic differential rating to that achieved when symbols were presented alone. This was most notable between signs 7 and 8. Sign 7 improved from 14th to 1st position when 'Falling rocks KILL!' was added to the pictorial image (Plate 8). Mean scores improved by 1:63 evaluative, 1.52 potency, 2.22 activity and 0.86 understandability.

The three signs that used words only in standard format (white letters on a red background; Plates 2, 11 and 14) all achieved ratings on the understandability factor of under 3.00; evaluative scores were also impressive all being less than 3.64. However, their performance was less satisfactory on potency and activity factors; all three mean scores for activity were over 4.00.

Discussion

The experiment examined the perceived effectiveness of 'new' symbolic and symbolic/worded signs, against that of two, word-only signs currently sited at the GHC. The ability of current signs to create awareness was not at question; 84% of users at Dunraven beach perceived the existing warning signs and 88% of users as a whole claimed to be aware of rockfall hazard (Williams & Williams 1988). At question, was their ability to prompt changes in user behaviour, as 86% of those who located within 30 m of the Dunraven cliffs had perceived the signs. (Williams & Williams 1988).

The semantic differential test found existing signs scored well on evaluative and understandability factors (Table 2) but less well on potency and activity. It is clear that current signs are easily understood and their design cannot be fully discounted as unsuitable.

SN	E	P	A	U	MS	OP
1	3.52	3.95	3.55	3.52	3.63	7
2	3.14	3.46	4.124	2.32	3.26	3
3	3.77	3.55	3.41	4.46	3.79	9
4	3.41	3.76	3.67	3.26	3.52	6
5	3.23	3.09	2.94	3.69	3.23	2
6	4.02	3.99	3.50	3.75	3.75	8
7	4.39	4.45	4.79	3.73	4.34	14
8	2.76	2.93	2.57	2.87	2.78	1
9	3.99	3.21	2.91	3.77	2.47	5
10	4.17	4.39	4.04	4.11	4.17	12
11	3.64	4.29	4.95	2.97	3.96	11
12	4.23	4.60	4.83	3.67	4.33	13
13	4.76	4.14	4.54	5.29	4.68	15
14	3.29	3.69	4.03	2.62	3.40	4
15	3.94	3.97	4.07	3.85	3.95	10

SN = Sign Number
E = Evaluative
P = Potency
A = Activity
U = Understandability
MS = Mean Score
OP = Overall Position

**Table 2 Mean Semantic Differential Scores
for Individual Signs**

However, their weakness is in changing behaviour. This
perhaps stems from the lack of potency and activity
identified; the signs may appear passive and bore
viewers. It was encouraging, therefore, to note that
several of the experimental designs not only scored well
on evaluative and understandability factors, but also on
potency and activity; in particular, Plates 5 and 8
(Table 2).

The widespread support of symbol usage offered by many
researchers (King, 1975; Dewar & Ells, 1977; Mackett-
Stout & Dewar, 1981), would appear to have credance.
However, it is in conjunction with words that this
medium is most effective (Table 3). Certainly the
Health and Safety executive make much use of this format
in hazard warning posters: for example, on AIDS,
smoking and accidents at work. However, in using
symbols, a certain degree of caution must be
administered; it is easy for ambiguity to creep into a

design and lead to confusion. Plate 13 usefully illustrates this point. In the fore-ground of the sign a bird is shown dislodging a loose block:- a familiar scenario at the GHC. In addition, a perspective view of the cliffs is represented. The cliffs detract perception away from the figure resulting in ambiguity.

This was evident not only from the high-mean scores obtained (5.29 understandability; Table 2) but also from comments made by participating test subjects. Easterby (1977) described this as a lack of symbol stability leading to a degradation of symbol value. Individuals seeing unstable images have to make a best-possible interpretation. This is influenced by the perceptual 'set' or expectations and assumptions acquired during the course of learning. In the experiment, the bird image was familiar; four rectangular blocks to present cliffs were not. Finally, the experimental signs produced do not represent perfected combinations of words and symbols. Equally good results may have been obtained with other varying combinations. More important than the actual designs was the fact that the experiments revealed alternatives to current word only signs that in laboratory tests were perceived to be more effective

Following the encouraging results obtained in the laboratory, an experiment to field test the highest ranked sign (Plate 8) was devised. A full-size warning sign measuring approximately 1 x 2 m was constructed from plywood and painted using the Plate 8 design. It was envisaged that the percentage number of users locating in an identified risk area at Dunraven beach would be monitored with the existing warning sign in position; then this sign would be replaced by the new sign and a similar monitoring exercise conducted to compare effect. For the experiment to be credible, it was necessary to remove the existing sign for approximately one week (depending upon the weather). However, Ogwr Borough Council refused permission to remove the sign, despite support from the GHC authority and Cook and Arkwright, the estate managers. Owing to this the experiment was abandoned.

This disturbing attitude contrasts the view of other UK local authorities who have welcomed and financed cliff hazard research: for example, Grainger and Kalaughers' (1988) work on the Devon coastline.

Sign Type	Sign Number	Evaluative	Potency	Activity	Understandability
S	1	3.52	3.93	3.55	3.52
S and W	6	4.02	3.99	3.50	3.50
Change	··········	+0.50	+0.06	-0.05	-0.02
S	7	4.39	4.45	4.79	3.73
S and W	8	2.76	2.93	2.57	2.87
Change	··········	-1.63	-1.52	-2.22	-0.86
S	12	4.23	4.60	4.83	3.67
S and W	4	3.41	3.76	3.67	3.26
Change	··········	-0.82	-0.84	-1.16	-0.41
S	10	4.17	4.39	4.04	4.11
S and W	15	3.94	3.97	4.07	3.85
Change	··········	-0.23	-0.42	+0.03	-0.26
S	13	4.76	4.14	4.54	5.29
S and W	3	3.77	3.55	3.41	4.46
Changes	··········	-0.99	-0.59	-1.13	-0.83

*Minus readings signify a drop in Semantic Differential Scores, indicating an increase in the perceived effectiveness of a sign.

S = Symbol   S and W = Symbol and Word

Table 3   Changes in the perceived effectiveness of five symbolic signs, when words were added

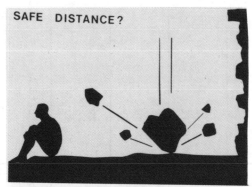

Plate 1

Plate 2

Plate 3

Plate 4

Plate 5

Plate 6

Plate 7

Plate 8

Plate 9

Plate 10

Plate 11

Plate 12

Plate 13

Plate 14

Plate 15

Conclusions

A semantic differential test was employed to determine the perceived effectiveness of fifteen hazard warning signs. The fifteen comprised of two word-only signs currently erected at the GHC and other experimental designs, using combinations of words and symbols. Current signs scored well in understandability and evaluative factors but less well on potency and activity (Table 2). New signs incorporating both words and symbols were perceived to be more effective (Plates 5 and 8).

Acknowledgements

The authors wish to thank the Nature Experience Learning Research Programme for providing the financial assistance which made work possible on this project. Also Keith Abbott and his co workers who provided the necessary logistical help and Claire Hooper for the typing.

References

COUNTRYSIDE   (1981)   Information   signs   for   the
COMMISSION   countryside.   CCP 132.

DEWAR R E &   (1977)   The   semantic differential as
ELLS J G   an   index   of   traffic sign
                                perception & comprehension.
                                Human   Factors,   19(2)
                                pp. 183-189.

EASTERBY RS   (1970)   The perception of symbols for
                                machine displays.   Ergonomics
                                13. pp. 149-158.

ELLS J G &   (1979)   Rapid comprehension of verbal
DEWAR R E   and symbolic traffic signs
                                messages. Human Factors, 21,
                                pp. 161-168.

KING L E   (1975)   Recognition   of symbol   and
                                word   traffic   signs. J of
                                Safety Res. June, 7(2) pp.
                                80-84.

MACKETT-STOUT J &   (1981)   Evaluation   of   symbolic
DEWAR R E   public   information   signs.
                                Human   Factors,   23(2),
                                pp. 139-151.

OSGOOD C E,   (1957)   The   measurement   of
SUCI G J &   meaning.   Urbana, Illionis
TANNENBAUM P H   Univ of Illinois press.

SZLICHICINSKI K P   (1979)   Telling   people   how   things
                                work.   Applied   Ergonomics
                                10(1), pp. 2-8.

A T WILLIAMS   (1987)   Coastal Conservation Policy
                                Development in England and
                                Wales with special reference
                                to   the   Heritage   Coast
                                concept. J Coastal Research,
                                31 (1), pp. 99-106.

A T WILLIAMS   (1987)   Rates   and   mechanisms   of
P DAVIES   coastal   cliff   erosion   in
                                Lower   Lias   rocks.   Coastal
                                Sediments '87 (ed) N C Kraus,
                                American   Society of Civil
                                Engineers, pp. 1855-1870.

M J WILLIAMS   (1988)   The   perception of,   and
A T WILLIAMS   adjustment   to,   rockfall
                                hazards along the Glamorgan
                                Heritage   Coast,   Wales,   UK.
                                Ocean & Shoreline Management,
                                11, pp. 319-339

The Case for Privatisation of Public Beach Facilities in a Developing Country

Colm P. Imbert[1]

Abstract

In keeping with global trends, the Government of Trinidad and Tobago, like many other Governments of developing countries burdened with high levels of public sector expenditure, is seeking to divest itself of several areas of economic activity formerly reserved for the State, including the maintenance and upkeep of public leisure areas, such as public beaches. Up to the present time, the Government has provided services and facilities at public beaches in Trinidad and Tobago, including car parking, first aid, lifeguards, rest rooms, beach cleaning, and so on, free of charge, or at a nominal fee. Financial constraints have now forced a re-examination of this policy.

The Government's first attempt to privatise the facilities at a popular public beach in Trinidad, Maracas Beach, in early 1990, met with a storm of public protest, and it was forced to back down on its original plans to hand over the management of the beach facilities to a private developer. Concerns raised ranged from environmental issues to questions about public access, public safety and security, and the terms and conditions of the proposed lease for the beach facilities.

This paper examines some of the emerging issues in the privatisation of Government services provided at public recreation areas, particularly public beaches, in a middle-income developing country (Trinidad and Tobago), and proposes a publicly acceptable system for the provision of public services and facilities at public beaches by the private sector.

---

[1]Lecturer in Civil Engineering, University of the West Indies, St. Augustine, Trinidad, W.I.

1.0 Introduction

Trinidad and Tobago is the southernmost country in the English-speaking Caribbean, and at its closest point is located some 10 kilometres (7 miles) off the North-Eastern coast of South America (see Figure 1a). It is an independent twin-island state with a total land area of 5,100 square kilometres (2,000 square miles). In 1990, the population stood at just over 1.2 million, giving an average population density of 235 people per square kilometre (600 people per square mile), with the vast majority of people (95%) residing in Trinidad. The population is cosmopolitan in nature with people of Negro and East Indian descent making up the bulk of the population. Trinidad and Tobago lies at approximately 11° North Latitude and 60° West Longitude. The climate is consequently a tropical marine type, and both islands are traversed by mountain ranges with flat hinterlands.

The economy throughout the years has been characterised by cyclical booms and depressions which have generally followed fluctuations in world market prices for primary products, such as sugar and crude oil. The economy is dominated by petroleum products, however, although progress has been made in the agricultural and industrial sectors. Per capita income has dropped considerably over the last 8 years, but the country is still classified as "middle-income developing" by international development institutions. There are several public beaches in both islands, many of which are maintained to some extent by the State, with varying levels of public services provided at these beaches by the State depending on the popularity of the individual beaches in question. The beach that is the subject of this study, Maracas Beach, is an extremely popular public beach, if not the most popular public beach in the main island of Trinidad, and every weekend, thousands of people make their way to the beach for recreation and relaxation.

Trinidad and Tobago was formerly a British colony. The country gained independence from the British in 1962, and achieved full republican status in 1976, with the recognition of the President as the Head of State. The country's present republican constitution is based on the British Westminster model, with a 36-member Lower House of Parliament, i.e. the House of Representatives, and a 31-member Upper House of Parliament, i.e. the Senate.

The House of Representatives is comprised of elected representatives who are elected on the first-past-the-post system at general elections held every five years. The Senate is made up of appointed members, comprising

FIGURE 1a - THE CARIBBEAN (PARTIAL MAP)

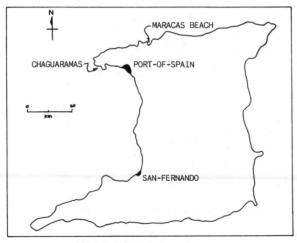

FIGURE 1b - TRINIDAD

15 Government Senators, 9 Independent Senators and 6 Opposition Senators.

In the Trinidad and Tobago Parliament, Government Ministers are required to answer questions posed to them on matters of public importance. In 1989 and 1990, the Government came in for heavy criticism for what appeared to members of the public to be its desire to move too abruptly and hastily from the existing status quo of State ownership and operation of public facilities to reliance on the private sector to provide services at public recreation areas. In the particular case of the public facilities at Maracas Beach, after the idea of privatisation was first raised in the Press, there were expressions of public concern, and an outcry by several independent journalists regarding what appeared to be virtually a "secret" or "undercover" State divestment operation.

A question on the Government's plans for privatisation of the public services provided by the State at the beach was subsequently lodged in the Senate (the Upper House of Parliament) in early 1990 by an Opposition Senator. The Government was asked to confirm whether it intended to lease the public facilities at the beach to a private developer, and if so, to give details of the proposed lease arrangements.

The Minister with responsibility for Tourism, under whose portfolio the maintenance and operation of public beach facilities fell, eventually replied to the question in the Senate some weeks later. It was revealed that as part of the Government's thrust towards divestment of the State's responsibility for public services, plans were already well advanced in early 1990 to lease the State's assets at Maracas Beach to a private company, and so transfer the responsibility for provision of public services at the beach from the Government to the private sector.

The proposed "privatisation" arrangements included leasing of the entire existing 6 hectare (15 acre) parcel of public beach front land at Maracas Beach, including all existing public access roads to the beach, and all the existing public facilities, such as changing rooms, car parks, restaurant facilities, and so on, to a private company for a 15-year period. It was also disclosed that during the period of the proposed lease, the private developer would be allowed to make improvements to the beach facilities, and charge user fees to the public for services provided, such as car parking, security, use of the beach for public or private functions. New beach facilities (e.g. swimming pools, a health and fitness club "on the beach", fast food distribution outlets) were also proposed. The private developer would be given overall control of the public facilities at the beach, and would be allowed to regulate the activities of the public at the beach.

After these proposed lease arrangements were announced, the public outcry intensified, and the Government was soon forced to reconsider its plans to "privatise" the services provided at the beach. The issues raised by members of the public covered a wide range of fears, misgivings, and apprehensions, which are found to be typically associated with current privatisation initiatives in developing countries (**Cook et al, 1989**).

Environmental issues, questions about restriction of public access to the beach, and about the ability of the private developer to fulfill the terms of the lease were foremost. In May, 1990, apparently giving in to public pressure, the Trinidad and Tobago Tourism Development Authority, which was the Government agency assigned to negotiate the lease arrangements for the beach facilities, terminated its negotiations with the private company, citing as grounds that the company had been unable to satisfy certain financial pre-requisites for the lease. Seven months later in December, 1990, in an almost complete turnabout, the Government announced that a new wholly State-owned company had been formed to maintain, develop, and manage the public facilities at Maracas Beach.

The idea of privatisation of the public services at the beach was thus temporarily abandoned by the Government.

Notwithstanding this final turn of events, this paper will seek to propose what could and should have been done in order to pursue a viable programme of privatisation of Government services at public beaches in a developing country such as Trinidad and Tobago.

2.0 The Beach

2.1 Physical characteristics

Maracas Beach is located on the mountainous North Coast of Trinidad (see Figure 1b), and is a typical horseshoe-type beach protected by rocky headlands. The bay in front of the Beach, Maracas Bay, is approximately 3 square kilometres (1 square mile) in plan area, and faces the southern Caribbean sea. The prevailing winds are the North-East trades, which set up moderate breakers from time to time, very suitable for body-surfing and other similar water-based leisure activities.

The shape and extent of the beach sand area follows a cyclical pattern, dependant to a large extent on the presence of storms and swell activity in the area. Movement of sand on and off the beach is typical for a horseshoe beach, with reduction of beach area and formation of an offshore bar during the winter months of December to February, which are usually characterised by storm and squalls, and growth in the sand area during the gentler summer months of June to August. The beach profile and grain size distribution of the beach sand also follows a cyclical pattern, with coarser sand grains and a steeper beach profile experienced during the winter months, and a gentler beach profile with finer sand grains experienced during the summer. This pattern of sand movement is, however, sometimes disturbed by the passage of tropical storms in the latter half of the year. The beach sand is mainly of quartz origin, and is usually light yellow or off-white in colour. The sea water in the bay is usually a clear greenish-blue colour, due to the presence of mild organic activity. The beach therefore provides a fine bathing area, and its flat foreshore a valuable public recreation area.

2.2 Historical development

Maracas Beach was not always public. Prior to World War II, when Trinidad and Tobago was a British colony, the beach formed part of 200 hectare (500 acre) private coconut estate, and access to the beach was generally restricted, since the only land access route was through private lands.

In 1942, the then colonial Government acquired the beach and several hectares of the surrounding land for public use, and a paved first-class road was built over the hills to the beach from Port-of-Spain, the capital city of Trinidad. The records of the time indicate that the road to the beach was constructed by the American Government, apparently as partial compensation for the lease of extensive waterfront lands on the North-West peninsula of Trinidad, in an area known as Chaguaramas, close to the western suburbs of Port-of-Spain. The United States built a major naval base in Chaguaramas during World War II, and the Chaguaramas waterfront area, which was previously a very popular public bathing and recreation site for people from all over Trinidad, was thus restricted from use by the Trinidad public.

Local historians are of the view that Maracas Beach was consequently opened up to the public in order to diffuse public displeasure at the loss of the highly valued Chaguaramas beaches.

The beach therefore has been in public use for nearly fifty years. After independence in 1962, and particularly in the 1970's and early 1980's, the public facilities at the beach were expanded considerably by the Trinidad and Tobago Government, and by 1986 these facilities included a first-aid station, lifeguard services, changing rooms, fresh water showers and toilets, two bars and a restaurant, several food vending stalls, three public car parks, beach cleaning and maintenance services, and so on. Services were provided free to the public or at minimal cost. As an example, use of the changing rooms and toilets at the beach was provided at a cost of TT10¢ (US2¢) per person, which hardly covered the cost of printing the admission tickets, far less the cost of providing personnel and upkeep and maintenance for the changing rooms.

Owing to financial constraints, brought about primarily by the decline of oil prices in 1982, and the eventual collapse of these prices in 1985, coupled with the onset of the global debt crisis in the early 1980's, the Government of Trinidad and Tobago, like many other developing nations at the time, was forced to reduce public expenditure in the middle-to-late 1980's. One of the areas that was most severely hit by budget cuts was the Trinidad and Tobago Tourist Board. This Tourist Board was later restructured into the Trinidad and Tobago Tourism Development Authority (TDA) in late 1987, after a new Government took office in December, 1986. Prior to 1987, the Tourist Board had been given responsibility and funds by the Government for maintenance and upkeep of several tourist attractions and public leisure areas, including public beaches. This responsibility was later assumed by the Tourism Development Authority

In keeping with the divestment thrust of the new Government at the time, the new Tourism Development Authority took steps to "privatise" the public services provided at Maracas Beach. In addition to budget cuts, the need to divest responsibility for the operation and upkeep of the public facilities at the beach was made more acute by the deteriorating condition of the facilities, which, due to worsening financial constraints, had not been kept in good condition for several years. In fact, by the time the lease arrangements were being negotiated in 1989, most of the public facilities at the beach had been badly vandalised, and were non-functional.

The Tourism Development Authority was, therefore, quite serious in its intention to divest itself of the responsibility for maintaining the facilities at the beach. When the "privatisation" issue became a matter of

national concern and focus in late 1989, it was revealed
that three private companies had been invited by what
the Government later termed a "public advertisement"
(although few people seemed to be aware of it) put out
by the Tourism Development Authority to tender for the
takeover of the beach facilities as far back as 1988,
acting on a Cabinet decision taken in 1987.

At the time of the so-called "public advertisement",
however, little notice was taken of these activities by
the public, and generally, the first stages of the
privatisation process for the beach facilities were not
taken seriously. In hindsight, it appears that the
general Trinidadian public did not think it possible
that the Government or any of its agencies would hand
over control of the most popular public beach in
Trinidad to a private developer without some form of
open public discussion and consensus, and so disregarded
the rumours of imminent privatisation of the services at
the beach.

3.0 The Government's "privatisation" proposal

All of the details of the proposed lease of the beach
facilities to a private developer were never fully
revealed by the Trinidad and Tobago Government before it
shelved its original privatisation plans. However,
public advertisements and interviews in the Press by the
proposed private developer and statements made in
Parliament by Government Ministers, allowed the
following points to emerge:

1. The lease of the beach facilities was to be for a 15-
   year period, and included lease of all the available
   land fronting the beach and all of the existing
   public facilities at the beach.

2. The private developer was to be given effective
   control of the public facilities at the beach, and
   could regulate the activities of the public at the
   beach.

3. The Government had agreed that the private developer
   could make what were described as "improvements" to
   the public facilities at the beach.

4. The private developer was to be allowed to charge
   user fees to the public for use of the facilities at
   the beach.

3.1 The public's concerns

When it first became apparent that the Government really intended to proceed with the "privatisation" of the facilities and services at the beach, a public outcry erupted. This outcry grew into a full-fledged protest in the national media, and eventually in the country's Parliament.

Questions were initially directed at the background and experience of the private company which was favoured to take over the management of the beach facilities. It was also felt that an issue as sensitive as the privatisation of the facilities and services at the most popular public beach in Trinidad should not be so far advanced in 1990 under what appeared to many people to be conditions of secrecy. Not very many people had heard of the proposed private developer, or were familiar with his track record in similar operations. The public protests increased when attempts by the developer to confirm his suitability, and to clear up doubts about the process of his selection, were met with skepticism in several quarters, particularly in the daily Press.

Questions were then directed at the developer's plans for takeover of the facilities and services at the beach, and one of the problems that emerged immediately was the question of responsibility for lifeguard services. It soon became apparent that this was a "gray area" in the proposed lease arrangements, since neither the Government nor the private developer seemed willing to accept responsibility for maintaining lifeguard services at the beach, once the beach was handed over. The private developer had apparently not catered for a substantial increase in his labour force, and indeed, the lifeguards were of the view that they would be retrenched once the beach was "privatised". Clearly, however, in a developing country such as Trinidad and Tobago, which has a tourist trade, one would not wish to have a public beach without lifeguards. Fortunately, this very serious area of public concern and safety was later satisfactorily resolved when the Government agreed publicly to maintain full responsibility for providing lifeguard services at all public beaches in the country, regardless of any lease arrangements or privatisation initiatives in the future.

The next contentious issue was environmental in nature. Prior to finalising the lease for the beach property, it was reported that the private developer had taken it upon himself to "restore" the beachfront to what was (erroneously) described as its "original" condition. This was said to have been achieved by moving sand from one area of the beach, which was experiencing accretion

at the time, to another area of the beach, which was
experiencing erosion. It was claimed that the beach was
"rebuilt" by this process. This raised a storm of
protest from local coastal engineers and ecologists, who
were of the view that the developer appeared to be
ignorant of the nature of the cyclical coastal processes
peculiar to the beach, and so might not possess the
required competence for maintenance of the beachfront
area. It was further argued that the developer could be
threatening the long-term stability and stable
vegetation line of the beach by unnecessarily removing
sand from an area which served as a natural source of
beach material during the period when the annual erosion
process switched from one side of the beach to the
other.

The developer's plans to "improve" the facilities and
services at the beach were queried next. It was reported
that the developer planned to construct an additional
paved car park for the beach, thus reducing the extent
of the grassed areas along the beachfront, in addition
to constructing a "health spa", a children's recreation
area, additional restaurants and bars, a swimming pool,
a craft market, catering to the tourist trade, and
several small regulated fast food distribution outlets.

Water sports such as jet skis and windsurfing were also
reported to be planned for the bay area. Vehicular
traffic to the beach, use of the beach for parties and
other similar functions, and the playing of games such
as football on the beach, were to be restricted. Several
traditional food vendors were to be relocated from their
existing locations on the beach, and the method of food
preparation and menu selection was to be regulated.
Security personnel were to be placed at the beach to
ensure that specific regulations for the conduct of the
public on the beach were to be followed.

The public's concerns about the proposed "improvements"
were multifaceted. Historically and culturally, Maracas
Beach had been associated for years with the preparation
and sale of certain local delicacies and foods, such as
"Maracas shark and bake" (a tasty combination of freshly
fried filet of shark in homemade pastry). Sale of this
and other similar local treats at the beach would
apparently not be encouraged under the new lease
arrangements, which seemed to cater more for the North
American pallet (e.g. hamburgers and hot dogs).

It was also felt that restriction of the type of games
and sports permissible at the beach was an infringement
of basic rights. The idea of restriction of public
access to the beach by a private developer was met with

a loud protest, since this was also considered to be an infringement of basic rights.

Several individuals were of the view that the "improved" beach would be much too commercialised, and that the beach would lose its natural unspoilt appeal. One letter writer to the newspapers described the developer's plans for "improving" the beach as an attempt to turn Maracas Beach in Trinidad into a replica of Miami Beach in Florida, USA, and indicated his displeasure with this idea in no uncertain terms. With regard to proposed water sports and other similar water-based activities in the bay, such as jet-ski rental, these too were met with a loud "no", because of possible injury to bathers, particularly children. In all of this, it must be remembered that Maracas Beach was the most popular public beach in the country, and was used by thousands of people on weekends, particularly families with small children.

The general consensus among the public, therefore, was that the facilities at the beach should be left basically unchanged, and that no further "improvements" should be made to them. It was generally felt that all that was required was proper refurbishment of the existing facilities.

It was also felt that the terms of the lease were far too generous in favour of the developer, and that he was being given control of extremely valuable and cherished public property at rates which were way below prevailing market rates for similar beach front properties.

4.0 Conclusions and recommendations

4.1 Conclusions

The attempt by the Trinidad and Tobago Government to privatise the public services at a public beach in 1990 was unsuccessful.

The initiative failed for many fundamental reasons.

In the first instance, the choice of public facility for privatisation, a very popular public beach, was far too visible and sensitive for a developing country such as Trinidad and Tobago, which prior to 1987 did not have a history of private sector provision of former Government services. The situation was made even more sensitive by the initial aura of secrecy which appeared to surround the deal, and which quite naturally led to deep suspicion of the true motives for the privatisation initiative. It was generally felt that the tender process for lease of the beach facilities was not sufficiently publicised, and that the public's views should have been sought beforehand.

It is now generally accepted by most advocates of privatisation that in order for it to be successful in developing countries, three factors are critical, namely 1. Public support 2. Government commitment and 3. Policy reform (**Elicker and Johnson, 1990**). In the case of privatisation of the Government facilities Maracas Beach, public support was withheld largely because of the suspicious nature of the lease arrangements. The extent of privatisation proposed, that is virtually complete divestment of State responsibility for the services provided at the beach, also led to apprehension and mistrust.

The terms of the proposed lease, particularly the annual rent to be paid by the private developer to the Government, were thought too be much too generous. A proposed initial annual rental figure of TT$10,000 (US$2,350) for the beach facilities was given by the Government in Parliament after questioning by members of the Parliamentary Opposition. This rental figure did not compare favourably with prevailing rental charges for similar public recreation areas in Trinidad, where rents for comparable properties were as much as 6 to 10 times more.

The situation was also not helped by the attitude adopted by the preferred private developer, who, rather than seeking to allay public fears about his competence, the apparently overly generous terms of the proposed lease, possible environmental damage to the beach, over-commercialisation of the beach facilities, and restriction of public access and enjoyment, sought instead to attack members of the public who voiced their objections to the privatisation proposals. In one case, a local newspaper columnist (**Imbert, 1990**) who had expressed serious concerns in the daily Press about the manner in which the lease arrangements for the takeover of the beach facilities was being conducted was threatened with libel action in the courts, if he did not retract his objections, and publish an apology.

Another problem with the Government's plans to "privatise" the services and facilities at the beach was its declared intention to lease the entire parcel of land surrounding the beach to the private developer, along with all the existing built facilities. This proposal raised the question of restriction of public access and egress, and also the question of Government abrogation of responsibility for public facilities. It was generally felt that if all of the beach land was leased to a private company, then the public might eventually be barred from using the beach.

The concept of a private developer taking over a long-established public car park at a public beach, and charging a user fee of his choice, was also not well received. The overriding fear was that the private developer would be given too much control over the public beach facilities and that the Government might not intervene in time if the public's basic rights, such as freedom of movement and association, were abused. As a result, it was generally felt that it would be safer to lease only the built physical facilities at the beach to a private company, and not the beach land itself.

The public's reaction to privatisation in the case of Maracas Beach thus emphasised the need for Governments in developing countries to move cautiously in new policy areas, and one of the Trinidad and Tobago Government's failings in this issue was its inability to reassure the public that certain basic norms, minimum standards, and quality of service, would be met by the private developer when the facilities at the beach were handed over. Such public misgivings are common in privatisation initiatives. As **Utt (1989)** puts it: **"Privatisation involves change, and change is often seen as a dangerous source of instability and loss...It is essential that public officials realise that privatisation is a political process with economic consequences...This means that the politics of the issue must be addressed first"**.

4.2 Recommendations

Although the Trinidad and Tobago Government abandoned its original plans to privatise the public facilities at Maracas Beach, several important points were raised during the public debate on the issue. The Trinidad public was not totally opposed to the idea of privatisation of the services provided by the Government at the beach. The general consensus was that people were willing to pay for public services provided by the private sector at a public beach, once certain specific guidelines and regulations were established.

The following is a summary of privatisation proposals which the author feels would have worked for Maracas Beach, if the Trinidad and Tobago Government had approached the issue with a bit more finesse:

1. A National Parks Authority, or similar umbrella organisation, should have been created to monitor, and, if necessary, regulate, the operations of

private developers at public recreation areas, such as public beaches. Such parkland Authorities are common in developed countries. All relevant park land belonging to the State could be vested in this Authority. Such an Authority would have the responsibility of regulating the level of user fees that could be charged for the use of public facilities, in consultation with private developers, and also for approving any development work to public property under its control.

2. "Carte blanche" leasing of State beach land to a private developer should have been avoided. The lease arrangements should have been confined to the buildings and other physical facilities, leaving the actual beachfront areas completely public.

3. Proper safeguards should have been taken to ensure that free public access and egress to the beach, and public enjoyment, were maintained at all times.

4. The privatisation exercise should have been conducted in the full view of the public, following recognised public tender procedures, and only after extensive public consultation had taken place.

5. Prevailing rates for lease of similar properties should have been charged, so as to avoid accusations of an "inside deal".

6. Traditional values and customs regarding use of the beach should have been accommodated, and given priority in any plans for improvement of the beach facilities.

It is important to note that the Trinidadian public was willing to go along with a measure of privatisation of the services provided by the Government at the beach. It was generally accepted that the public facilities had deteriorated due to financial constraints, and also that it was difficult for the Government to improve the level of services offered at the beach without assistance from the private sector. But the privatisation exercise was badly handled, and suspicion about the motives and competence of the private developer took root. This could have been avoided.

References

1. Cook, P. and Kirkpatrick, C., Editors, "Privatisation in Less Developed Countries", St. Martin's Press, NY, 1989, Conference Proceedings.

2. Elicker, P. and Johnson, G.O.F., "The Global Sweep of Privatisation", Economic Impact, No. 70, 1990

3. Utt, R.D., "Privatization: Shifting the Balance Toward Growth", International Health and Development, 1989, also Economic Impact, No. 69, 1989

4. Imbert, C.P., "The Secret Privatisation of Maracas Beach", Trinidad Guardian Newspaper, March, 1990

Oil Pollution in Jamaica's Coastal Environment

Margaret A.J. Jones[1] and Peter R. Bacon[2]
Zoology Department
University of the West Indies
Mona Campus, Kingston 7, Jamaica W.I.

Abstract

A study was carried out between December 1987 and February 1989 in order to determine the state of petroleum hydrocarbon contamination (oil pollution) in Jamaica's coastal environment. This assessment was done by the analysis of four parameters which assessed the occurrence and levels of different forms of petroleum hydrocarbon residues. These were the analysis of surface slicks/sheens; dissolved/dispersed petroleum hydrocarbons (DDPH) in the water column; pelagic tar balls and stranded beach tar.

Residues were collected from twenty-nine beach stations and six sea stations over the study period with monthly visits to beach stations and quarterly visits to sea stations.

Eleven slicks/sheens were observed over the fifteen month period and DDPH was detected in 100% of the samples with values ranging from 0.59 to 34.60 μg l^{-1}. Pelagic tar was found in 10.3% of samples with values ranging from 0 to 109 mg m^{-2}. Beach tar was the most prevalent and persistent form of contamination showing a very clear pattern of distribution. Values of beach tar ranged from 0 to 11.940 g m^{-1}. The east coast and Kingston Harbour are subjected to constant relatively large amounts of fresh tar; the north coast was impacted by a large spill about four years ago (1986); the west coast is virtually clean, while, the south coast (excluding Kingston Harbour and environs) recorded no beach tar at any time.

----

[1]Senior Technical Information Officer.Scientific Research Council Hope. Kingston 6. Jamaica W.I.
[2]Senior Lecturer. Zoology Department. U.W.I., Mona, Jamaica W.I.

Introduction

Since 1979 the Intergovernmental Oceanographic Commission's Regional Commission for the Caribbean and Adjacent Regions (IOCARIBE) has conducted a monitoring programme for petroleum pollution in the Wider Caribbean Region. The programme was implemented within the IOCARIBE marine pollution research and monitoring programme, CARIPOL. The CARIPOL programme in Jamaica was carried out in Kingston Harbour (Provan, 1985) its Approaches (Gillett, 1985) and along some south eastern beaches (Wade et al, 1987).

This study was carried out as a means of continuing the CARIPOL data base for Jamaica using the techniques and methodologies recommended by CARIPOL. Four parameters were analysed: slicks/sheens, dissolved/dispersed petroleum hydrocarbons (DDPH) in the water column, pelagic (floating) tar and stranded beach tar.

Materials and Methods

Slicks/Sheens

All slicks/sheens that were observed or publicly reported were recorded over the fifteen month period, October 1987 to February 1989. Where possible visual quantification of the size and extent was done according to IOCARIBE (1980) and UNESCO (1984) guidelines. Information was collected island-wide.

Dissolved/Dispersed Petroleum Hydrocarbon (DDPH)

Six sea stations (Fig. 1) were chosen for the collection of seawater samples for analysis of DDPH. Samples of seawater were collected in 4 litre solvent bottles. The sample bottles were placed in an aluminum frame bottle holder to which was attached a receiving line with a float 1m above the bottle. This ensured that all samples were collected 1m below the surface.

The seawater samples were extracted with two 50 ml aliquots of redistilled nanograde hexane (IOCARIBE, 1980; UNESCO, 1984) dried with a few grams of sodium sulphate (Na_2SO_4) and 2 ml of mercuric chloride solution added to prevent microbial degradation. The hexane extract was then reduced in volume by rotary evaporation to 5 ml. The extracts were analysed by spectrofluorometry (Jones, 1989a).

The values of DDPH met the assumptions underlying parametric tests and statistical analysis of the levels detected was carried out using the Analysis of Variance Random Block Design (Sokal and Rohlf, 1981) to test for significance between levels by site and by month.

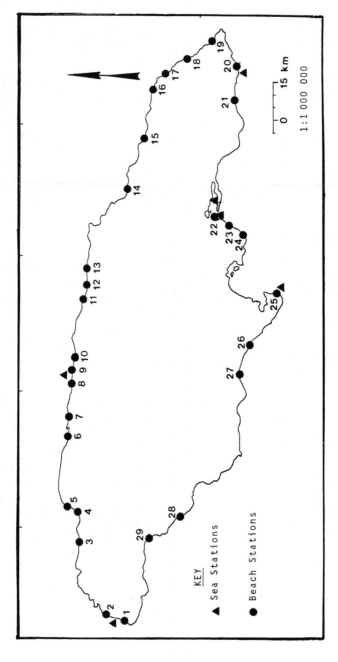

Figure 1: Map of Jamaica showing six sea stations and twenty-nine beach stations

Pelagic (Floating) Tar

Pelagic tar was collected at the same time as the seawater samples for analysis of DDPH. and at the same stations. Pelagic tar was sampled with a neuston net supported by a vinyl pipe frame with dimensions 1.0 m x 0.5 m and net mesh of 1.0 mm. The net was towed at 1 knot for 15 minutes. in a circle to increase the homogeneity of the sample. The tar collected was weighed after removal of debris (Jones. 1989a) and the quantity calculated as mg m^{-2}.

Beach Tar

A preliminary survey of the Jamaican coastline was carried out in November 1987 in order to locate suitable beach stations according to specifications set out by CARIPOL (IOCARIBE, 1980: UNESCO; 1984). From this survey twenty-nine beach stations were chosen (Figure 1). Beach tar was sampled once a month over the period December 1987 to December 1988. All beach sites were visited monthly as beach tar has been shown to be the best indicator of persistent oil pollution.

At each beach transect lines of 1m width were run from the water line to the backshore where the first signs of stable vegetation began and all visible pieces of tar were collected. taken back to the laboratory and weighed after extraction of extraneous material (Jones. 1989a). and the tar recorded as g m^{-1} of beach front. The beaches were not cleaned after each sampling period and tar collected was not thrown back so that tar collected was a combination of older persistent. as well as freshly deposited tar.

Beach tar was statistically analysed using the Friedman Two-Way Analysis by Ranks for Randomised Blocks followed by multiple comparison.

Results

Slicks/Sheens

Eleven slicks/sheens were observed and/or reported over the 15 month period and showed no spatial or temporal restrictions (Table 1). There were 5 reported in Kingston Harbour, 2 in Hunt's Bay. 1 at Alligator Pond in St. Elizabeth, 1 at Discovery Bay in St. Ann and 1 at San San Beach in Portland. Damage ranged from fouling of fishermen's gear to fish kills and economic losses up to J$430,000 were reported from one incident.

Table 1: Slicks/sheens recorded over the study period (Source: Jones, 1989a)

LOCATION	DATE	EXTENT OF DAMAGE
Kingston Harbour	22/9/87	Fouling of boats, fishing gear; loss estimated at J$430,000; extensive fish kill.
Kingston Harbour	10/87	Fish kill; approx. 1,000 gals. of heavy crude;
Kingston Harbour	4/5/88	No report of extent; waste water released from factory.
Alligator Pond	22/11/88	No reports on size of spill or extent of damage.
Kingston Harbour	3/8/88	Chocolate mousse and sheens reported; thought to be from a ship.
Kingston Harbour	20/8/88	Bunker C from a hotel pipeline no information on extent.
Discovery Bay	8/88	Oil slick sighted, later identified as crude; no reports on damage.
Kingston Harbour	2/9/88	Seepage from power barge; high mortality of crustaceans; hundreds of metres of shoreline soiled.
Kingston Harbour	5/10/88	Mangrove roots covered as much as 9 cm; dimensions of slick approx 400 m by 75 m.
San San Beach	20/1/89	Tourists observed and reported slick while swimming; oil adhered to skin and bathing suits.

Dissolved/Dispersed Petroleum Hydrocarbons (DDPH)

100% of the samples collected contained detectable levels of
DDPH.   The levels of DDPH (Table 2. Figure 2) ranged from
$0.50 \mu g$ l^{-1} at Negril in June 1988 to 34.6 μg l^{-1} in the Middle
Harbour (S_4) in December 1988. All levels recorded at all sites
were below 10 μg l^{-1}. which is the average for the Wider
Caribbean Region (Atwood. et al 1987) with the exception of the
Middle Harbour which recorded levels an order of magnitude higher
in 60% of the samples.

Statistical analysis of the DDPH levels indicated a significant
difference in the levels found at sample sites (P<0.05) with the
Middle Harbour having a mean that was significantly higher than
all other sites.   However. there was no significant difference
among the means of the other sites. The levels of DDPH detected
showed no significant difference by month.

Pelagic (Floating) Tar

Pelagic tar was found in only 10.3% of the samples (Table 3).
twice in Kingston Harbour. once at Discovery Bay and once at
Barnswell. Pelagic tar residues were rare and irregular in
occurrence.   The residues detected at Discovery Bay were in
February 1988 and 1989 when the seas were extremely rough and
debris was observed in wind driven currents.   The residues in
Kingston Harbour occurred as finely dispersed droplets while
fresh semi-solid lumps were collected at Barnswell. The levels
of pelagic tar ranged from 0 on most visits to 109.9 mg m^{-2} at
Barnswell.

Beach Tar

A total of 332 visits were made to the beach stations and tar was
found on 40% of the visits (Table 4). The occurrence of tar was
found to be consistent with regard to spatial and temporal
influences with some sites consistently recording high levels of
tar and other sites consistently recording no tar at all.   The
levels of beach tar ranged from nil at 10 sites to over
11,000 g m^{-1} at Discovery Bay. The levels of beach tar produced
non-normal, highly skewed distributions. Statistical analysis by
non-parametric tests indicated a high level of significance
(P<0.001) by site.   The means for each beach station were
calculated and a qualitative analysis was done based on these
means (Figure 3) assigning each site to a class as follows:

> No Contamination (0 g m^{-1})
> Mild Contamination (> 0 $\leq$ 40 g m^{-1})
> Moderate Contamination (> 40 $\leq$ 100 g m^{-1})
> Heavy Contamination (> 100 $\leq$ 500 g m^{-1})
> Gross Contamination (> 500 g m^{-1}).

Table 2 : Levels of dissolved/dispersed petroleum hydrocarbons ($\mu g \; l^{-1}$) at six sea stations during the period February 1988 to February 1989

Site Number and Name	Feb	Jun	Aug	Dec	Feb	Total	Mean	S. D.
1 Negril	2.61	0.59	1.05	1.44	--	5.69	1.42	0.75
9 Discovery Bay	4.82	1.53	1.33	3.58	7.72	18.98	3.80	2.35
20 Bowden	4.07	2.90	1.05	2.01	9.28	19.31	3.86	2.89
22a Kgn. Harbour S_4	15.27	10.27	2.35	34.60	8.56	71.05	14.21	11.00
22b Kgn. Harbour S_2	4.35	4.17	6.04	2.24	3.07	19.87	3.97	1.29
25 Barnswell	6.63	2.31	3.99	5.61	--	18.51	4.63	1.64
Total	37.75	21.77	15.81	49.48	28.63	153.44	--	--
Mean	6.29	3.63	2.64	8.25	7.16	--	--	--
S. D.	4.19	3.17	1.84	11.86	2.42	--	--	--

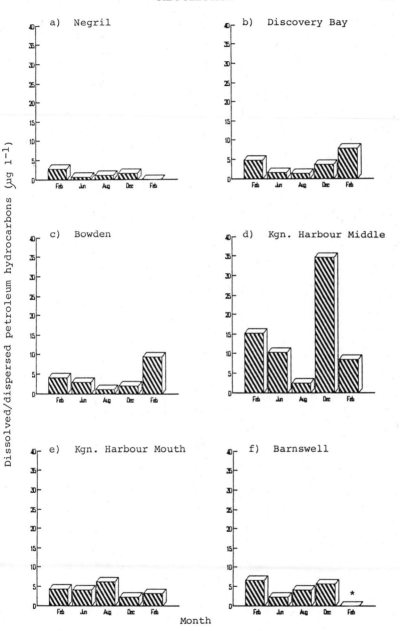

Figure 2: Levels of DDFH (μg l^{-1}) for six sea stations

Table 3 : Levels of pelagic tar (mg m^{-2}) at six sea stations during the period February 1988 to February 1989

Site Number and Name	Feb	Jun	Aug	Dec	Feb
1 Negril	0	0	0	0	–
9 Discovery Bay	36.3	0	0	0	25.0
20 Bowden	0	0	0	0	0
22a Kgn. Harbour S_4	0	2.2	0	0	0
22b Kgn. Harbour S_2	0	0	0	0	0
25 Barnswell	0	109.9	0	0	–

Table 4: Levels of beach tar (g m-1) detected at twenty-nine beach stations (and two off-shore cays)

Site Number and Name	Dec	Jan	Feb	Mar	Apr	May	Jun	Jul	Aug	Sep	Oct	Dec	Total	Mean	S.D.
1. Negril	0	0	37.0	0	0	0	0	0	0	0	0	0	37.0	3.1	10.2
2. Bloody Bay	0	0	0	0	0	0	0	0	0	0	0	0	0	0	0
3. Sandy Bay	0	0	38.2	0	0	0	12.4	0	0	0	0	0	50.6	4.2	10.8
4. Montego Freeport	0	0	0	0	0	0	4.3	0	13.4	0	0	0	17.7	1.5	3.8
5. Montego Airport	0	0	0	0	0	0	0	0	0	0	0	0	0	0	0
6. Falmouth	.0	0	0	0	5.4	0	0	0	0	0	0	0	5.4	0.4	1.5
7. Burwood	369.1	937.6	376.7	358.8	24.9	100.1	105.4	770.7	546.6	0	0	0	3589.9	299.2	306.4
8. Rio Bueno	194.1	1950.2	2113.1	332.8	393.8	250.0	102.6	223.0	37.4	0	0	0	5597.0	466.4	712.1
9. Discovery Bay	7208.4	1769.0	11940.1	4079.6	3894.5	5321.5	6838.5	4553.7	4075.4	605.0	1020.0	1093.6	52399.3	4366.6	3104.9
10. Pear Tree Bottom	193.1	401.2	90.6	23.5	58.3	30.7	10.4	250.5	10.9	0	0	0	1069.2	89.1	122.2
11. Priory	23.6	308.2	9.7	28.4	7.3	8.4	8.7	23.5	4.5	0	0	22.3	444.6	37.1	82.3
12. Mammee Bay	10.9	1.5	8.1	13.8	33.2	10.1	9.4	10.5	7.3	0	0	3.6	108.4	9.1	8.5
13. Ocho Rios	0	0	13.1	0	0	0	0	0	0	0	0	0	13.1	1.1	3.6
14. Annotto Bay	0	0	0	0	0	0	0	0	0	0	0	0	0	0	0
15. Hope Bay	0	0	0	0	0	0	0	0	0	0	0	0	0	0	0
16. Blue Hole	1.8	0	270.2	14.0	19.2	5.0	0	0	0	0	-	-	310.2	31.0	73.9
17. Long Bay	0	0	31.9	2.9	5.9	32.0	0	0	0	0	-	-	72.7	6.1	11.7
18. Manchioneal	-	-	-	-	-	-	-	-	20.6	86.1	51.3	59.4	217.4	54.4	23.4
19. Holland Bay	54.2	19.8	229.7	130.3	65.8	497.8	278.6	507.5	186.0	95.9	104.2	122.8	2292.6	191.5	156.0
20. Bowden	0	0	0	0	0	0	0	0	0	0	0	0	0	0	0
21. Lyssons	0	0	0	0	0	0	0	0	0	0	0	0	0	0	0

Site Number and Name	Dec	Jan	Feb	Mar	Apr	May	Jun	Jul	Aug	Sep	Oct	Dec	Total	Mean	S.D.
22. Kgn. Harbour B:	0.6	0	0.4	3.2	-	-	-	-	-	-	-	-	4.2	1.4	1.3
23. Salt Pond Beach	20.2	105.4	0.9	25.2	120.5	19.6	150.0	13.2	7.0	77.9	118.5	52.9	711.3	59.3	50.4
24. Wreck Point	-	-	-	-	-	-	-	-	10.2	-	-	-	10.2	-	-
25. Barnswell	56.0	268.6	432.6	256.1	754.0	802.9	753.3	191.5	192.7	65.2	101.1	118.2	3992.2	332.7	271.2
26. Gut River	0	0	0	0	0	0	0	0	0	0	0	0	0	0	0
27. Alligator Pond	0	0	0	0	0	0	0	0	0	0	0	0	0	0	0
28. Parker's Bay	0	0	0	0	0	0	0	0	0	0	0	0	0	0	0
29. Bluefields	0	0	0	0	0	0	0	0	0	0	0	0	0	0	0
30. Morant Cays (L)	-	-	-	-	-	59.3	-	-	-	-	-	-	59.3	-	-
31. Morant Cays (W)	-	-	-	-	-	910.3	-	-	-	-	-	-	910.3	-	-
Total	8132.0	5761.5	15592.3	5268.6	5382.2	8047.7	8273.6	6544.1	5112.0	930.1	1395.1	1472.8	71912.6	-	-
Mean	301.2	213.3	577.5	195.2	207.0	309.5	318.2	251.7	196.6	34.5	53.7	56.7	-	-	-
S.D.	1333.7	506.3	2264.8	768.3	54.5	1013.6	1312.9	879.0	757.1	115.6	196.4	210.2	-	-	-

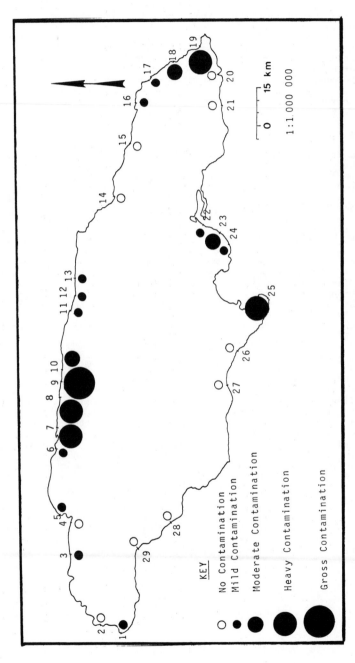

Figure 3: Qualitative analysis of beach tar contamination based on mean levels

By month, it was found that the levels of beach tar detected over the period December 1987 to August 1988 are significantly higher (P < 0.001) than those detected over the period September to December 1988 (Jones & Bacon, 1990). This is due to the occurrence of Hurricane Gilbert in September 1988. Although statistical tests show a significant difference in overall levels of tar detected before and after Hurricane Gilbert, it has been shown that the contaminated beaches were restricted to three main areas before the hurricane and remained restricted to these same areas after the hurricane (Jones, 1989b).

Discussion

The most persistent and visual form of petroleum hydrocarbon residue in the Jamaican coastal environment was stranded beach tar, while pelagic tar residues appeared to be irregular in occurrence. Slicks/sheens were not restricted to any particular area over the study period and DDPH was the only parameter which was detected at all sampling stations at each sample period.

The waters of the west coast had low levels of DDPH as indicated by the consistently low values detected at Negril. The west coast is the leeward coast of Jamaica and as such in not impacted by the Caribbean Current, while the westward flowing waters tend to constantly move material away from the coastline. This factor is reflected in the absence of stranded beach tar and pelagic tar along the west coast. As expected, Kingston Harbour had the highest levels of DDPH due to local influences such as the PETROJAM oil refinery, the high level of shipping activity in the Harbour and shore based industries utilising crude oil (Provan, 1985; Provan et al, 1987).

The detected levels of beach tar give the most vivid indication of the state of oil pollution in Jamaica. Discovery Bay and surrounding beaches appeared to have been impacted by a particulary large spill from a passing tanker sometime in 1986, the effects of which were still evident. In addition, to fresh tar at these sites there was the persistance of large quantities of tar from that incident. The east coast sites also have a severe beach tar problem. At each sampling period fresh tar balls were found, indicating that the east coast is receiving a regular supply of fresh oil. This is expected on this windward coast of Jamaica exposed to the prevailing North East Trade Winds and the Caribbean Current. Such coasts have been shown to be more contaminated than leeward coasts (Atwood, et al 1987). The source is likely to be ships utilising the Windward Passage that release oil accidentally or deliberately (Wade et al, 1987). The south coast beaches (excluding Kingston Harbour and environs) recorded no beach tar at any time, but the slick recorded at Alligator Pond is an indication that this coast is also susceptible to contamination from oil pollution.

The occurrence of beach tar on Jamaican beaches should be of concern in light of the dependence of the Jamaican economy on tourism. A factor such as beach tar contamination will reduce the aesthetic appeal and recreational usage of beaches. It has been shown (Atwood et al. 1987) that when values of beach tar reach 10 g m^{-1} beach users get soiled by tar and at values approaching 100 g m^{-1} beaches become virtually unusable for tourist purposes. This fact should be noted by the Jamaican tourist industry since, of all the beaches that recorded tar at any time, over 30% of them recording levels more than or approaching 100 g m^{-1}.

APPENDIX 1

References

Atwood. D.K., F.J. Burton. J.E. Corredor. G.R. Harvey. A.J. Mata-
    Jimenez. A. Vasquez-Botello and B.A. Wade (1987). Results
    of the CARIPOL Petroleum Pollution Monitoring Project in the
    Wider Caribbean. Mar. Pol. Bull. 18(10):540-548.

Gillett. V.. (1985). An Evaluation of Oil Pollution in the
    Coastal Waters of the Approaches to Kingston Harbour,
    Jamaica, during 1980-1982. M. Phil. Thesis, Zoology Dept.,
    University of the West Indies. Mona, Jamaica: 156 pp.

IOCARIBE (1980). CARIPOL Manual for Petroleum Pollution
    Monitoring: 20 pp.

Jones. M.A.J. (1989a). An Evaluation of the Status of Oil
    Pollution in the Jamaican Coastal Environment. M. Phil.
    Thesis. Zoology Dept., University of the West Indies. Mona:
    239 pp.

Jones. M.A.J. (1989b). Effect of Hurricane Gilbert on Beaches
    and the Status of Coastal Oil Pollution: 55-59 In Bacon.
    P.R. (Ed.) Assessment of the Economic Impacts of Hurricane
    Gilbert on Coastal and Marine Resources in Jamaica. UNEP
    Regional Seas Reports and Studies No. 110: 78 pp.

Jones. M.A.J. and P.R. Bacon (1990). Beach Tar Contamination in
    Jamaica. Mar. pol. Bull. 21(7):331-334.

Provan. M. (1985). The Status of Oil Pollution in Kingston
    Harbour. M. Phil. Thesis. Zoology Dept., University of the
    West Indies. Mona. Jamaica: 184 pp.

Provan. M.. B. Wade. A. Mansingh and E. Roberts (1987). Origin.
    Nature and Effects of Oil Pollution in Kingston Harbour.
    Jamaica. Carib. J. Sci. 23(1):105-113.

Sokal. R.R. and F.J. Rohlf (1981). Biometry. W.H. Freeman and
    Co. New York: 859 pp.

UNESCO (1984). Manual for Monitoring Oil and Dissolved/Dispersed
    Petroleum Hydrocarbons in Marine Waters and on Beaches.
    Intergovernmental Oceanographic Commission Manuals and
    Guides. No. 13: 35 pp.

Wade. B., M. Provan, V. Gillett and P. Carroll (1987). Oil
    Pollution of Jamaican Coastal Waters and Beaches: Results of
    the IOCARIBE/CARIPOL Monitoring Programme (Jamaica) 1980-
    1983. Carib. J. Sci. 23(1):93-104.

THE GROUNDING OF SHIPPING CONTAINERS IN THE BRITISH VIRGIN ISLANDS

Jessica Blok-Meeuwig[1]

ABSTRACT

On 2 November 1989, the Panamanian-registered ship 'Mar' sank 15 miles N.E. of Anguilla, West Indies, while on route from St.Maarten to Spain. The ship was under tow, carrying a cargo of 51 C.T.I. shipping containers. The entire cargo was lost in the incident and by 5 December 1989, nine containers had washed aground in the British Virgin Islands (B.V.I.).

All nine containers were carrying bobbins of industrial thread. The thread was 100% cotton and spun onto cardboard or plastic spools and the bobbins were individually wrapped in plastic bags. These bobbins presented a hazard to the marine environment as they damaged the seabed and the plastic could potentially cause death in sea turtles.

A clean-up operation was instigated by the Conservation and Fisheries Department of the B.V.I. Government. The Department also undertook an assessment of the environmental damage.

1. INTRODUCTION

The British Virgin Islands (B.V.I.) are a group of over 60 islands located 60 miles east of Puerto Rico, West Indies. In 1982, the contribution of marine-based tourism to the GDP was estimated to be 57.3% (Gold et al., 1985). Given that the economy of the B.V.I. is largely dependent on pristine waters and beautiful beaches, it is necessary to ensure that pollution and damage to the marine environment are minimized.

On 2 November 1989, the Panamanian-registered ship 'Mar' sank 15 miles N.E. of Anguilla while on route from St. Maarten to Spain. The ship was under tow and carrying a cargo of 51 C.T.I. shipping containers. The entire cargo was lost in the incident. By 5 December 1989, nine containers had washed ashore in the B.V.I. All of these containers were carrying bobbins of industrial thread, measuring 8 inches in diameter. The thread was 100% cotton

---

[1] Dalhousie University, School for Resource and Environmental Studies, 1312 Robie St., Halifax, N.S. Canada, B3H 3EC.

and spun onto cardboard or plastic spools. Each bobbin was individually wrapped in a plastic bag. The containers and bobbins presented a hazard to the marine environment as they damaged the seabed and the plastic coverings could potentially cause death in sea turtles.

This paper describes the containers, the clean-up operation and associated costs, and the ecological damage to the coastal and marine environment resulting from the incident.

2. THE CONTAINERS

The nine containers were located at Dead Chest Island (DC), Mosquito Island (MI), Eustatia Island (EI), Horseshoe Reef (HS 1 & HS 2), and along the northern coast of Anegada at Cow Wreck Bay (CW), Bones Bight (BB), Cooper Rock (CR) and Pelican Point (PP) (Figure 1). Seven of the containers measured 20'*8'*8' and contained approximately 6,000 bobbins each. The remaining two containers measured 40'*8'*8' and contained approximately 12,000 bobbins each.

3. ENVIRONMENTAL CLEAN-UP AND COSTS

The clean up operation was begun by the Conservation and Fisheries Department of the Ministry of Natural Resources and Labour, B.V.I. Government. The owners of the ship 'Mar' hired the company, West Indies Transport to complete the clean-up and removal of the containers.

Initial surveillance was carried out by staff from the Conservation and Fisheries Department. Several trips were made to the containers located at Dead Chest Island, Eustatia and Mosquito Island and the two on the Horseshoe Reef. The containers were inspected to see if they were intact and the sea bed was surveyed by snorkelling to assess the damage resulting from the containers and bobbins. Video footage of damage done to the reef by the containers was taken using an underwater video camera and damage was recorded. The shoreline was also inspected to determine how many of the bobbins were washing ashore.

The four containers on the north side of Anegada were not accessible by boat due to the barrier reef running along the north shore of the island, extensive shallows and high ground seas. Thus, these sites were visited by helicopter. At each site, Conservation and Fisheries staff were put down on the containers, enabling them to inspect the containers and the surrounding seabed.

Subsequent surveillance trips were made by boat to

investigate reports of containers breaking open or being opened by unauthorized persons. During March, 1990, the Conservation Office also made attempts to monitor the salvage operation of West Indies Transport. The company, however, refused to allow any staff on board their vessel. The total cost of surveillance was $1,925.00.

The clean-up operation took place in several stages. The initial damage control and clean-up was done by the Conservation and Fisheries Department. At Dead Chest Island, where the doors of the container had been opened by unauthorized persons, the clean up consisted of several teams of SCUBA divers picking up bobbins and masses of unravelled thread from the seabed to prevent further destruction of benthic fauna. Volunteers helped clean up the shore by removing the bobbins from the wash zone and piling them up above the high water mark to be burned once dry. The reef on the north side of the island, down current from the container, was also checked for thread by divers.

The clean-up of the North Sound occurred in two stages. The two containers, at Eustatia and Mosquito Islands, had not broken open. Instead, an unknown individual had cut into the tops of both containers with a blow torch to see whether the contents were worth salvaging. Thus, the majority of the bobbins had remained inside. As the containers were too heavy to be removed with their waterlogged contents, a work crew of ten, under the direction of Conservation and Fisheries Department staff, unloaded the containers, bobbin by bobbin. Approximately half of the bobbins in the container at Eustatia Island were unloaded and the bobbins were transported to the village dock by a small barge. They were then loaded into a garbage truck to be transported to the dump on Virgin Gorda. This method was found to be too slow due to a variety of transportation difficulties.

It was then decided that a large barge from the main island, Tortola, would be more efficient. In the interim however, the container at Eustatia, significantly lightened, broke open, releasing most of the remaining cargo into the sea. The majority of these bobbins washed ashore on Eustatia Island, where they were removed by the work crew. The bobbins that sank to the seabed near the container were picked up by snorkelers and loaded onto the barge. Inside the container, SCUBA equipment was used to collect the remaining bobbins.

The container at Mosquito island had to be cut into as there was not enough room to unload it through the previously cut hole. The barge was brought along-side the container and all the bobbins were loaded onto the barge. The barge then carried the bobbins from both containers back to Tortola where they were condemned, loaded into

large trucks and taken to the dump. The container from
Mosquito Island was towed back to Road Town by the barge.

The clean-up operation in Anegada and the Horseshoe
Reef consisted of cleaning the beaches at Cooper Rock and
Cow Wreck Bay where large numbers of bobbins had washed
ashore from the containers that had broken open at Bones
Bight and Cooper Rock. No work was done on the actual
containers due to their inaccessibility and the lack of
appropriate equipment.

West Indies Transport removed the empty containers at
Dead Chest Island and Eustatia Island in February and
March, 1990. The company also removed the containers and
contents on the Horseshoe Reef and at Cow Wreck Bay.
However, the containers at Bones Bight, Cooper Rock and
Pelican Point were not removed by West Indies Transport as
expected and, in fact, broke open due to high ground seas.
The removal of the empty containers was deemed unnecessary
as they were resting on a rocky bottom; removal would have
been costly and would have damaged the barrier reef. The
total cost of the entire operation to the Conservation and
Fisheries Department was U.S. $12,678.39.

The beaches from Pelican Point to the eastern point of
Anegada and at Cow Wreck and Bones Bight require more clean
up work as bobbins were still floating in and polluting the
beaches as late as April. Furthermore, many of the bobbins
that initially floated in were buried in the sand. As these
beaches erode in the summer, these bobbins will be
uncovered and require removal.

4.   ECOLOGICAL DAMAGE

Ecological damage from the container groundings was
divided into 4 categories: damage to the seabed from the
container; damage to the seabed from thread; damage to the
shoreline; damage to the marine environment from plastic
bags.

   a. Damage to the seabed from the container.

As the containers were pushed ashore, they damaged the
seabed. Soft corals were ripped from the seabed. Hard
corals had branches broken off (i.e. Elkhorn coral,
Acropora palmata) or were shattered into small pieces (i.e.
Brain coral, Diploria spp.). Where the containers came to
rest, hard corals were ground down by the movement of the
container as it was shifted back and forth by wave action.
Depending on the size and species of the colony, and rate
of recolonization, replacement may take several decades
(Gittings & Bright, 1988). Seagrass beds were disrupted and
rubble habitat was flattened, resulting in the loss of
cryptic habitats and the dependent fauna.

b. Damage to the seabed and benthic fauna from the thread.

When the bobbins escaped from the container, they floated until becoming waterlogged. Once waterlogged, the bobbins sank to the bottom, where they unravelled, forming dense mats of thread. Soft corals and sea fans were ripped from the seabed. Branching corals were broken and mobile benthic invertebrates like sea urchins, Diadema antillarum, became so entangled they could not escape. There was also some damage to hard corals from smothering and surface abrasion.

c. Damage to the shoreline.

The main cause of damage along the shoreline occurred when mangroves became entangled in the thread and plastic bags. This was unsightly and extremely labour intensive to clean.

d. Damage to the marine environment from plastic bags.

The Leatherback Turtle, Dermochelys coriacea, which is endangered world wide, mistakes plastic for its favoured food item, jellyfish. Once ingested, the plastic bags can cause the turtle's death (Wilber, 1987).

The damage to the marine and shore environment at the sites varied according to the nature of the seabed and the distance from the container to the shore. In all cases except Dead Chest Island, where the container washed on to the shore due to the surrounding deep water, there was damage to the sea bed from the container. At Mosquito Island, the container ploughed through a seagrass bed. At Eustatia Island, the container came to rest on sand and healthy coral colonies. On the Horseshoe Reef, the containers at HS 1 and HS 2 destroyed rubble and in the latter case, living coral as well. The four containers on the north side of Anegada came to rest primarily on rock and seagrass, the substrate typically found in areas of high wave action.

The thread caused major damage to the seabed only in the two areas with live reefs and where the bobbins remained close to the containers: Dead Chest Island and Eustatia Island. At HS 2, there was live reef but the majority of bobbins were blown ashore by the wind before they became waterlogged enough to sink and unravel. Thus there was almost no damage to coral from thread at this site.

The damage to the shoreline was extensive on the eastern point of Anegada where the bobbins from HS 2 and the Pelican Point containers were washed ashore and entangled in the mangroves. As the area is only accessible by small boat, removal of the thread would required too much time and effort.

Plastic bags from seven of the nine containers were released to the marine environment. In the cases of Mosquito Island and HS 2, very few plastic bags were lost. However the other containers, Dead Chest Island, Eustatia Island, Bones Bight, Cooper Rock and Pelican Point, released all of their plastic bags to the marine environment (Table 1).

Table 1: Summary of damage to the marine environment from the containers and cargo.						
Site	H.C. (#)	S.C. (#)	S.G. (m^2)	Rb. (m^2)	P.B. (#)	Sh. (m^2)
Dead Chest I.	13	9	0	0	6000	0
Eustatia I.	18	12	0	0	6000	0
Mosquito I.	0	0	23	0	100	0
Horseshoe 1	0	0	0	74	0	0
Horseshoe 2	16	0	0	14	450	834
Cow Wreck Bay	0	0	0	14	0	0
Bones Bight	0	0	0	14	6000	0
Cooper Rock	0	0	0	14	6000	0
Pelican Point	0	0	0	29	12000	0

Note: H.C.= hard coral; S.C.= soft coral; S.G.= seagrass; Rb.= rubble; P.B.= plastic bags; Sh.= shoreline; #= number of coral colonies or plastic bags.

5. CONCLUSION

Despite the seemingly innocuous nature of the C.T.I. shipping containers and their non-toxic contents, the cost of a clean-up operation to the B.V.I. Government has been significant. The Government of the B.V.I. spent $12,678.39 not including the time of the Conservation and Fisheries Department staff who had to be moved from other designated work and the time of volunteers.

Furthermore, the cost of the environmental damage must be taken into account. Thread has been sited from almost one end of the territory to the either; from Anegada to Norman Island to the north coast of St. Thomas, U.S.V.I. There was also an unconfirmed report that two sea turtles were found entangled in thread (Boulon, pers. comm.). The two containers in the North Sound were the focus of much concern by the hotel and dive operators in the area due to complaints by patrons (Ryan, pers. comm.). The containers on the Horseshoe Reef polluted the richest coral habitat in the area which supports much of the B.V.I.'s fishing industry.

In the past, compensation for environmental damage was

not sought. However, with increased public awareness and concern in the scientific community and the escalating number of cases of marine pollution, ecological damage is now being assessed and compensation sought (Defoor & Mattson, 1985). This has been further facilitated through improved environmental legislation, and court decisions that found in favour of the environment. The U.S Oil Pollution Act (1990) provides a mandate for government agencies to promulgate regulations for the assessment of damages to natural resources resulting from oil pollution. The grounding of the M/V Wellwood on Molasses Reef in the Key Largo National Marine Sanctuary is one of the better known examples of compensation for environmental damages. The out of court settlement awarded the U.S. federal government $6.3 million in fines and damages (Bondareff, 1988).

Despite these advances, compensation for environmental damage remains a very controversial topic. One of the main problems is the lack of agreement on a methodology for resource valuation. The problem of compensation is of particular significance in developing countries which may lack the human resources to assess the damage and the legislative framework to hold the polluters liable. Countries like the B.V.I. are also highly dependent on their natural resources thus very vulnerable to this type of incident. The grounding of the C.T.I. containers is a prime example of a seemingly minor accident resulting in a significant level of environmental degradation. It is important then that appropriate methods for resource valuation in developing countries are designed and that a legal framework in which polluters can be held liable is created.

REFERENCES:

Bondareff, J.M. 1988. The M/V Wellwood grounding: the legal issues. Oceanus 31(1): 44-6.

Boulon, R., U.S. Fish and Wildlife, St. Thomas, U.S.V.I.

DeFoor, J.A. & Mattson, J.S. 1985. Restitution law and natural resource restoration bill: a mechanism to slow destruction of Florida's natural resources. J. Land Use & Environmental Law 1(3): 1-15.

Gittings, S.R & Bright, T.J. 1988. The M/V Wellwood grounding: the science. Oceanus 31(1): 36-41.

Gold, E.; Letalik, N.G.; Mitchell, C.L.; Simmons, D.A.; Underwood, P.C. 1985. Management and utilization of the marine resources of the British Virgin Islands. Halifax: Dalhousie Ocean Studies Programme.

Ryan, M. Manager, Bitter End Yacht Club, British Virgin

Islands.

Wilber, R.J. 1987. Plastics in the North Atlantic. _Oceanus_.
30(3): 61-68.

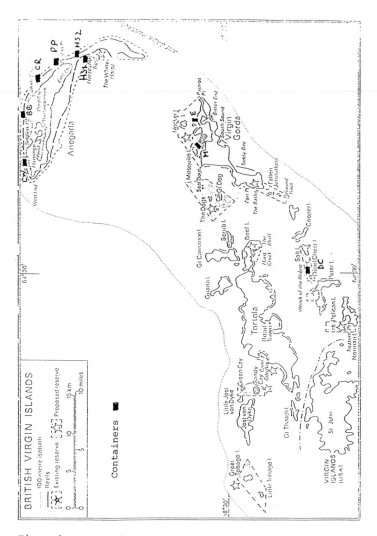

Figure 1: Map showing locations of shipping containers.

The Economic and Environmental
Consideration of Beach Sand Mining in
St. Lucia, West Indies

Kenneth M. Green[1]
and
Gillian Cambers[2]

Abstract

        This report focuses on the issues surrounding
the problem of beach sand mining today in St. Lucia.
The use of beach sand as a fine aggregate in the
construction industry is detailed and the associated
problems of beach sand extraction discussed. The need
to   sustain   a   healthy   construction   industry   is
recognized, but at the same time attention is drawn to
the negative impacts of this process. The available
statistics generated by Government reports indicate
that the demand for fine aggregate has grown steadily
during the past decade. An overview of the block
manufacturing industry including raw materials and
production costs is provided.

        Numerous options are available to provide the
construction industry with alternative sources of fine
aggregate without compromising the quality of the
concrete product. These options discussed in the
report include offshore dredging, sand importation,
pumice   importation   from   Martinique   and   pumice
production in St. Lucia. In summary, all of the
latter activities are deemed viable with the exception
of offshore dredging because of its considerable
negative environmental impacts.

----

[1]Presently, Senior Environmental Scientist, Vigyan
Research Associates, 5109 Leesburg Pike, Suite 807,
Falls Church, VA   22041.   Formerly, Project Chief,
Organization of American States, St. Lucia.

[2]Conservation   Officer,   Conservation   and   Fisheries
Department, British Virgin Islands.

Introduction

Beach sand mining has been a traditional source of fine aggregate for use in the concrete construction industry for many decades in St. Lucia and throughout the Caribbean. This natural resource also plays an important role in the long term stability of the island's beaches. Recent studies have concluded that extraction of beach sand causes considerable degradation to beach fronts, natural dunes and berms that serve as physical barriers to natural hazards such as sea swells and hurricanes. This can be translated today into economic concern about the future growth of St. Lucia's tourism gold mine. Continued sand mining will surely result in the deterioration and destruction of numerous beaches. These beaches will become less attractive for future hotel development sites since beautiful white sand beaches and abundant sunshine are the prime attractions to the tourism marketplace.

Natural Resources of St. Lucia

St. Lucia belongs to the Windward Island Group of the Lesser Antilles in the West Indies, and is situated between Martinique, 25 miles (40 km) to the North, and St. Vincent, 20 miles (32 km) to the south and is bound by latitude 13o42'N and longitude 60o52'and 61o05'W. The island is pear-shaped, measures 27 miles (43 km) by 14 miles (22 km) and covers an area of roughly 238 sq. miles (617 km2).

It is a deeply dissected mountainous island. The topography is dominated by a central mountain ridge which runs almost through its entire length and rises in the south-west at Mt. Gimie to a height of 3145 feet (950m) above sea-level. The mountain ridges are cut by many gullies giving rise to a dense drainage pattern and very steep slopes in the central area.

St. Lucia consists chiefly of volcanic rocks belonging to the Tertiary and Quarternary age with a few small sedimentary beds and coral reefs along the coastal tract. The volcanics comprise lava flows of basalt, andesite, dacite, agglomerates, tuff, ash and pumice (both andestic and dacitic). The basalts are believed to have crystallized from primary magma and andesites and dacites are derived mainly from the partial melting of crustal material. Based on age similarities, the rocks can be classified into a Northern, Central and Southern series.

In terms of tonnage, sand and gravel aggregate are now the two most important materials extracted in St. Lucia. Sand and gravel are required for use in the construction and building industry in St. Lucia and are in great demand. Other requirements include gravel for road beds, macadam preparations and sand for plastering i.e. rendering. Knowledge on the nature and distribution of these mineral resources in St. Lucia is critically important. In short, the continued growth of the construction industry will increase resource demand.

In St. Lucia there is no natural inland deposits of sand and the primary source of sand is from the land coastal interface of the island (approximately 32.6 km of beachfront). The second much smaller source of sand is found along several relatively narrow and short rivers (e.g. Piaye and L'Ivrogne Rivers).

Coastal Process and Form

The most significant natural phenomena impacting beach sand formation in St. Lucia and other Leeward and Windward coastal islands of the Caribbean is wave action. The East coast, being the windward side of the island, is considered a high energy coast with nearshore wave heights, commonly 1 meter. The leeward west coast receives considerably lower wave energy in the order of .15 to .3 meters nearshore (Cambers 1990).

Between the months of June and November, the major swells are associated with tropical storms and hurricanes that pass from east, in the Atlantic, to west across the Caribbean region. Hurricanes that pass directly over St. Lucia are of course concentrated energy impacts. The two major hurricanes of 1989, Hugo and Gabriella caused significant beach sand accretion and displacement. Seas as high as 10 meters were observed crashing onto shore on the leeward side of the island (pers obs.). Although these hurricanes hit the islands several hundred kilometers to the north of St. Lucia, the coastal impacts to St. Lucia were considerable.

The near and offshore reef formations are also important beach protection structures. Offshore reefs help displace the sea swells and reduce the wave energy as the wave moves toward shore. The largest and most active are fringing reefs off the northwest and southeast coasts. There are smaller patch reefs mainly on the western and northeastern coasts.

Beach Assesments

Work by Deane et al. (1973) and Cambers (1990) report on the status of St. Lucia's beaches. The recent field visits by Cambers in 1989 included details about road access, beach length, sand mining, and existence of development behind the beach. In summary, the 67 beaches in St. Lucia have a total length of 32.63 kilometers. Of these beaches, more than 30 % have been mined during the past twenty years. In terms of beach length, this accounts for more than half of the estimated beach front of the island. This figure represents beach mining status, but does not account for amount of sand extracted or location within each beach of sand mining.

Cambers determined, by subjective professional evaluation, that of the 20 beaches undergoing recent sand extraction, that only 6 beaches should be considered for large scale sand mining. Experts agree that the continued mining of these beaches on a large scale will result in significant beach erosion. The debate as to how much sand can be extracted from these mining locations continues.

Sand Mining

The traditional fine aggregate throughout the West Indies has been beach sand. In times past, the quantity of sand removed from beaches was small because of the widespread use of wood in construction. However, during the 1950's and 1960's decreasing endemic supplies of lumber from preferred tree species (e.g. green heart, white cedar, gome etc.) made building with local lumber more expensive and put supplies in greater demand. This situation, combined with more readily available imported cement, gradually resulted in greater concrete construction and parallel demands for fine aggregates.

The removal of sand from St. Lucia's coasts for use as fine aggregate has occurred for decades. The extraction and use of this renewable resource in construction is believed by numerous sources to have been accelerating dramatically in the past ten years. The scale of sand mining is linked directly to the strong economy and associated demand for residential homes, small to medium scale industry, larger construction projects and tourism development.

Beach sand extraction in St. Lucia occurs at both "regulated" and unregulated beaches. The Ministry of Communication and Works (MCW) issues permits to truckers, from the Chief Engineer's office, for specific amounts of sand. During 1989, these permits were issued officially for five beaches.

Government officials and the public in general, know full-well that sand is mined on a regular basis without permits from both permitted and non-permitted beaches. This beach sand mining has occurred for decades and remains virtually uncontrolled today. Trucks with 5 to 15 cubic yard capacity are brought directly onto the beach to collect sand. The most common practice is for local laborers to load the sand onto the trucks manually with shovels. Generally, 2 to 4 laborers can load a 5 cubic yard truck in 15 to 20 minutes. At certain beaches (e.g. Trou Salle and Fond D'Or) a front end loader is used to speed up the loading process to five minutes.

Collection of River Sand is a very different process. Individuals build piles of sand along the roadside adjacent to the specific river that sand is collected from. Usually, it is women who use 1-2 cubic foot baskets to haul sand from various locations along the River bed to their roadside pile. Truckers haul this river sand on an as available basis to specific block making operations.

Fine Aggregate Demand

Assimilating precise data to quantify demand is difficult but several demand "indicators" can be analyzed. Estimates of the annual amount of sand removed from beaches are based on a combination of professional knowledge, beach evaluation and review of available Government reports and statistics. Earlier studies estimating volumes of sand mining were synthesized by Williams (1985). In a 1972 study, Deane and his associates reported that 91,000 cubic yards of sand were removed from six beaches between 1960 and 1962. The most significant impact was the removal of an estimated 70,000 cubic yards from the Viegie Beach alone, during that period.

These researchers also concluded that three beaches on the northwest coast (Viegie, Choc, and Reduit), had 329,00 cubic yards of sand mined between 1960 and 1970 which represented slightly more than half of the total sand mined throughout St. Lucia for that 11 year period. The estimated total of beach sand mined based

on these studies was 572,000 cubic yards, which
translates to an average of 52,000 cubic yards per
annum.

More recent estimates of sand extraction have
been developed from reviewing Government reports.
Information provided from the MCW detailing the
permitted amount of sand extracted from beaches and
rivers for 10 months in 1989 yielded a total of 12,108
cubic yards. Extrapolating this figure for the year
yields approximately 15,000 cubic yards of permitted
sand, for both beaches and rivers. Review of the
permit figures and knowledge of sand extraction
processes on the island suggest that non-beach sand
(inland river) accounts for no more than 5% of this
total. In the final analysis, then, we can conclude
that 14,000 cubic yards were legally extracted during
1989. The validity of this information is brought
into question by examining in detail, statistics from
one permitted beach, Fond D'Or, on the east coast.
(See below.)

Other sources of information useful for
determining the amount of fine aggregate used in St.
Lucia include the approved annual concrete floor
space, sand and cement importation records. A
detailed discussion of these features is provided
elsewhere (Green, 1990). The major conclusion is that
construction activity in 1989 doubled from the early
1980's and the estimated demand of fine aggregate for
reported building applications was close to 100,000
cubic yards per annum. Since numerous residential
construction activities are undertaken in rural areas
without planning approval, it would be reasonable to
conclude that all forms of construction require as
much as 150,000 cubic yards of sand per annum.

Beach Sand Mining at Fond D'or Bay

Fond D'or Beach, located on the central portion
of the east coast just north of the town of Dennery
served as a major source of beach sand during the last
several years. Reasons for this concentration of
resource mining from this beach include; good access
to the main highway, a location served by the best
road on the island "near" to the capital city of
Castries and the heavily developed region of the
northwest coast and a beach front containing large
amounts of sand.

Statistics generated by staff from the Mabouya
Valley Development Project (a Ministry of Agriculture

land reform project located in the same valley as Fond D'or beach) provide useful information. In 1988, 22,973 cubic yards of sand were reported mined at Fond D'or, by an estimated 5743 truckloads (based on an average of 4 cubic yds per truck), yielding 43,000 US dollars in receipts (generated at permit price of 1.85 US dollars per cubic yard). Official FARMCO records suggest that the Fond D'or Beach generates 40% more fine aggregate than estimated via MCW information for all of the island.

Observations at Fond D"or and other beaches indicate that peak mining activities can easily produce 10 truck loads per hour, with manual loading. Assuming an 8 hour working day, it is likely that 80 trucks a day load at Fond D'or. This projected level of extraction would mean 400 trucks a week or over 19,000 trucks per year. An average truck load of 4 cubic yards yields an estimate of 76,800 cubic yards per annum of sand just from Fond D"or. When mechanical loading is used (which occurred frequently in Fond D'or) this estimate adjusts dramatically upward. One can conclude that with high demand, Fond D'or could have been producing as much as 100,000 cubic yards of sand per annum in 1988 and 1989.

Construction Industry Profile

Information on the construction industry was obtained by interviewing major and medium size construction companies in St. Lucia. In general, blocks used for construction were either purchased locally or made locally by the construction companies.

All the large construction companies indicated that they manufactured their own concrete using both local and imported raw materials. In the case of Higgs and Hill, 7740 cubic yards of concrete were made using coarse aggregate from Vieux-Fort and sand and cement from Trinidad. Kier International, gave an estimated usage of 20,000 cubic yards per year along with a yearly purchase of about 15000 bags of cement. Cement bought by the smaller construction companies ranged from 300 (Constantine's) - 5,000 (Gibbs) bags per month.

It was generally felt that the local blocks did not meet the building requirements of the construction companies. Builders maintained that the blocks were below specific minimum crushing strength and that they were not consistent and were expensive relative to their quality. From discussions with some of the smaller construction companies, it was felt that blocks made from river sand were stronger. However, it should be noted that river sand is not as readily available as beach sand.

Block Manufacturing

Many small and medium block manufacturers operate islandwide. Of the nine interviewed, the period of time in existence ranged from 1 to 6 years. About 50 percent of these operations had been established for just about 1 year. In all of these operations, the basic equipment used included moulds, shovels and wheel-barrows.

The amount of sand used by the large manufacturers ranged from 25 to 220 cubic yards per week. For the small and medium manufacturers the amount of sand used ranged from 5 to 10 cubic yard per week, with an average of 8 cubic yards.

Economic Considerations

In 1990, 5 cubic yards of beach sand delivered to Castries cost the consumer 93 US dollars, or slightly more than 18 US dollars a cubic yard. When used in concrete block manufacturing, this fine aggregate is mixed with coarse aggregate and cement. The 1990 prices for these raw materials cost the consumer around 38 US dollars, plus transportation costs. The fixed costs (1990 prices) for getting beach sand to a block plant in Castries was approximately 25.80 US dollars per cubic yard. Additional operational fixed costs include labor and equipment for making the blocks. These expenses have been calculated for a medium sized block manufacturer producing 2,500, 6" and 8" blocks per day.Operational labor expenses include 5 labourers, 2 drivers, and 2 handymen with additional investment costs required for the following equipment, 1 shed, 2 hand mixers, 1 block making machine and 2 trucks (3 and 5 cubic yard capacity each).

Many of the small block manufactures do not keep accounts for their business and the cost of producing a block could not be readily given. Costs were generated by estimating raw material costs and operating costs as discussed previously. The cost of producing a 4" block ranged from $US 0.28 - $0.45; for a 6" block it cost between $US 0.35 and $0.41 and for an 8" bock it cost from $US 0.41 to $0.52. It should be noted that the cost per block depended on the type and proportion of materials used, the cost of transportation and the cost of labour.

The retail price of blocks from the various manufacturers has also been analyzed. It can be seen that the price of a 4" block ranges from $US 0.45 - $0.65, for a 6" block from $US 0.54 - $0.74 and 8" from $US 0.82 - $0.93. In all except one case these prices do not include transportation cost.

The demand for blocks in St. Lucia is very high given the present nature of the construction industry. For 1989, a medium sized operation quoted a figure of 10,000 blocks being sold monthly. Further, all three large manufacturers pointed out that their supply had not met the demand. In all cases the large manufacturers are looking to increase production.

Further economic consideration must be given to the fact that current block making and demand results in blocks being shipped without proper curing. In fact, several contractors have said that as much as 50% of their purchased blocks easily break or are unusable by the time the blocks are used in building. Hence, it is reasonable to say, then, that under current conditions the "usable" blocks cost the contractor/consumer close to double the cost of one block or $US 1.60-$1.80 per 8" block. We will return to this feature later since it is extremely important when considering the concept of sustainable development and existing block manufacturing in St. Lucia.

Alternative Sources of Fine Aggregate

An undeniable conclusion is that present beach sand mining practices and river sand sources will be in increasing demand as the island's construction sector continues its strong growth. From the perspective of a supply and demand feature, there will need to be alternative sources of fine aggregate. Four specific alternatives will be considered; offshore dredging, sand importation, pumice importation from Martinique and development of a pumice mining industry in St. Lucia.

Offshore dredging

An evaluation of potential offshore sand deposits was undertaken by Deane et al. (1973). This study concluded that the total quantity of dredgable offshore sand was small (approximately 150,000 cubic yards) and did not justify offshore dredging operations.

An additional concern in evaluating this alternative is the potential environmental impacts of offshore dredging. These impacts include: accelerated erosion of the shoreline by higher wave action if the borrow area is sited nearshore; damage to existing reefs which function as natural breakwaters and producers of sand; physical damage and possible destruction of the bottom substrate that effects coastal fauna and flora; possible damage to mangroves; and problems of increased turibidity and sediment.

In light of the high cost of equipment required to dredge the limited volumes of offshore sand along the northwestern coast of St. Lucia and the probable serious negative environmental impacts discussed above, this source of sand is considered an unfeasible alternative.

<u>Sand importation</u>

As mentioned earlier, large scale construction projects have been given permission by GOSL to import bulk quantities of sand. In recent years, the Cul de Sac power station (Higgs and Hill), government building complex (Kier) and Coast Guard Station (Kier) have been constructed with fine aggregate from Trinidad. Several sand quarry operations are being operated in the northeast of the island of Trinidad with sand being transported by road to port destinations on the east coast for loading onto barges for shipping north to St. Lucia. The cost at 1990 prices, is approximately $24.00 US dollars per cubic yard delivered dockside in St. Lucia.

Another foreign source of sand for use as fine aggregate is Guyana. Several studies have been undertaken in Guyana to determine the feasibility of extracting the extensive inland geologic white sand series. These regosols and latosols cover an area estimated to be over 25,000 square kilometers dominating the northeast region of the country. The thickness of these deposits vary between 15 to 150 meters. These aggregates are composed of white quartz sand ("white sand") and brown loamy sand to sandy clay ("brown sand"). One recent proposal has been to collect sand from the upper reaches of the Esseqibo River as a by product of pumping the river bottom sediment for gold exploration. Presently, fine aggregate demand for the construction industry in

Georgetown is being met with sand being extracted from the white sand deposits within 50-60 miles of the city. Numerous economic and environmental issues would have to be explored in more detail to determine the feasibility of setting up a large scale sand export operation in Guyana. Nonetheless, this alternative source of sand can most certainly be imported into the Eastern Caribbean at a far cheaper price than todays Trinidad's price.

Pumice importation from Martinique

The island of Martinique, which lies 35 kilometers north of St. Lucia, contains very similar volcanic deposits. The island construction industry must adhere to French Federal building standards, because it is a French Province. Consequently, contractors and the building industry recognized in the yearly part of the 1980's that use of beach sand as a fine aggregate would not meet the existing French Government standards. Consequently, one of the larger mining company's (primarily coarse aggregate) on the island began to mine pumice from the northwest part of the island near the town of St. Pierre. This industry has flourished during the past six years and the company executives have explored market opportunities in St. Lucia. At the time of the writing of this report, product and delivery costs were not available. It is likely that the cost of this product extracted and delivered portside in bulk would still be less than sand from Trinidad.

Pumice

The fourth alternative source of fine aggregate is pumice from St. Lucia. The quality and volume of pumice on St. Lucia is sufficient to meet the demand of fine aggregate for several decades. Other factors that require consideration include the distribution of deposits in relation to transport corridors, ease of extraction, and environmental impacts from mining. Past studies have demonstrated conclusively that pumice is an excellent substitute for beach sand in making concrete. Strength tests of blocks made with pumice indicated these blocks are significantly stronger and of better quality (due to the absence of silica and chlorides). Furthermore, a new pumice mining venture was started in St. Lucia in August 1990 by two local businessmen. Two hotel projects have been buying the product and using it as fine aggregate in place of beach sand for all their construction activities. An existing constraint has been the difficulty in meeting demand. The cost for this product is $9.30US per cubic yard at the mining site or $18.60 per cubic yard delivered to Castries.

Conclusions and Recommendations

The preceding discussions accentuate the need to reduce beach sand mining in St. Lucia while providing viable alternatives for fine aggregate supply. Although eliminating the use of beach sand might seem necessary, it is considered impracticle at this time, given the existing difficulties with enforcement today on the island. Consequently, we recommend: encouragement of sand importation from Trinidad and pumice from Martinique; promotion and assistance to the infant pumice industry on the island; creation of a comprehensive incentive program that encourages use of alternative fine aggregates; and a public awareness and technology transfer program aimed at the public and the construction industry.

Appendix

References Cited

Cambers, G. 1990. Beach sand mining in St. Lucia. Organization of American States, Washington, D.C.

Deane, Compton, M. Thom and H. Edmunds. 1972. Report on first year's operation (1970-71). Regional Beach Erosion Control Programme, University of the West Indies (St. Augustine), Trinidad.

Deane, C.M. Thom, and H. Edmunds. 1973. Eastern Caribbean coastal investigations, 1970-1973. British Development Division/University of the West Indies (St. Augustine), Trinidad. 5 volumes.

Green, K. 1990. Beach sand mining in St. Lucia, a technical and economic analysis of demand and feasibility alternatives. Unpubl. report. The World Bank.

Williams, M.C. 1985. Beach sand mining in St. Lucia. EIA Workshop in the Eastern Caribbean, CCA, Barbados.

Hydrogeology of Caribbean Coral Reef Islands

Daniel W. Urish[1] M., ASCE

Abstract

The small coral reef islands of Carrie Bow Cay and South Water Cay receive sufficient groundwater recharge to develop fresh water lenses in accordance with the Ghyben-Herzberg principle. The climate, tidal effect and hydrogeology of both islands are the same with the landmasses differing only in size. Thus, the effect of size in fresh water lens formation can be isolated. On tiny Carrie Bow Cay with a width of only 38 meters, a very thin fresh water layer of a few centimeters forms in the wet season, while on South Water Cay with a width of 100 meters, a fresh water layer almost one meter thick develops. During the dry season only a brackish water transition zone exists on Carrie Bow Cay and the fresh water layer on South Water Cay shrinks to about 0.5 meter.

Introduction

Oceanic landmasses under natural water table conditions commonly develop a body of fresh ground water. This fresh water body assumes the form of a lens floating on the saltier and denser underlying seawater. It is thickest in the central part of the landmass tapering to a thin edge at the shore margins. In general, the groundwater flows from the thickest part of the lens outward and upward to the shoreline. The magnitude of the fresh water lens depends primarily on landmass size and configuration, permeability, groundwater recharge and tidal conditions.

The sister islands of Carrie Bow Cay and South Water Cay lie 24 kilometers off the Central American Mainland on the edge of the Belizean Barrier Reef in the Caribbean Sea (Figure 1). Separated by only 1.5

[1] Associate Professor, Civil and Environmental Engineering, University of Rhode Island, Kingston, RI 02881

kilometers of seawater they share common climatic, hydrologic and tidal conditions. They do, however, differ significantly in size with South Water Cay having 16 times the land area of Carrie Bow Cay (Figure 2). This difference affords the opportunity to investigate the independent effect of island size on fresh water lens formation while the other principal factors remain the same.

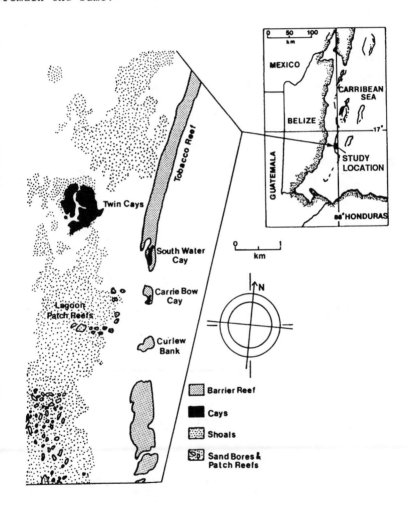

Figure 1.   Location of Study Area (after Rutzler and Macintyre,1982)

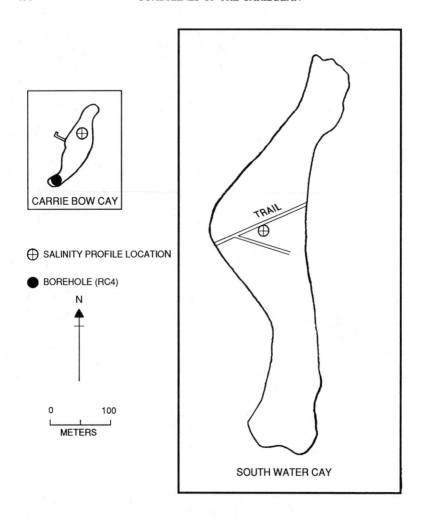

Figure 2. Plan View of Carrie Bow Cay and South Water Cay (after Stoddart, et al, 1982).

During the period of January, 1987 through January, 1990, as a part of the Smithsonian Institution Carribean Coral Reef Ecosystem Program, field investigations were conducted to determine the nature of groundwater systems in the islands. During this period subsurface soil borings were made and monitor wells installed to obtain hydrogeologic and water quality information. Groundwater sampling was done both at the end of the wet season in January when a fresh water lens was thickest, and in May at the end of the dry season when lens thickness is at a minimum.

Carrie Bow Cay (16 48' N, 88 05'W)

Carrie Bow Cay is a small kidney shaped island with an area of about 0.4 ha a length of about 100 m and a maximum width of only 38 m. The land surface is flat with a maximum topographic elevation of less than 1.0 meter above mean sea level. Originally the island was covered by bushes 20 feet high and fringed by mangrove trees, but was altered by man beginning in the 1900s to a coconut palm woodland (Stoddart, et al, 1982). Now the ground surface is sparsely covered with low vegetation interspered between coconut palm trees. In the 1940s the mangrove fringe was cleared to rid the island of insects. This action alleviated the insect problem, but also removed the protective barrier against sea erosion. Since clearing of the mangroves, the island has become smaller with each passing storm.

The island is the site of the Smithsonian Institution Reseach Station for Belizean Barrier Reef research studies. A large part of the island is covered by research support buildings. Roof runoff concentration, rainfall catchment systems, and washwater disposal tend to distort the shape of the delicate fresh water lens from a natural configuration.

For Carrie Bow Cay even a limited ephemeral fresh water lens is important to the ecosystem both for sustaining the island vegetation as well as being a determinate of the nature of the environment at the near shore margin of the island where groundwater seepage occurs.

South Water Cay (16 49'N, 88 05' W)

South Water Cay is the largest inhabited sand cay of the islands of the Belizean Barrier Reef. It has an area of about 6.49 ha, a length of 660 meters and widths varying from 55 to 175 meters (Stoddard et al, 1982). The island is flat with a slight depression in the center. Its maximum topography is about 1 meter above mean sea level. The coastline is subjected to significant erosion during storms.

The island is covered by a coconut palm woodland with parts of the island covered by dense grass and brush thicket where development has not altered it. In areas where development has taken place, the ground has

been cleared to bare sand. Garbage disposal pits as well
as shallow dug wells dot the island. Currently, for
water quality reasons, residents rely more on roof
catchment water than on groundwater. Frequently,
however, during the spring dry season water shortages
become a problem.

The importance of South Water Cay to mariners
sailing along the barrier reef is underscored by its
name identifying it as a watering station. The
significance of the water supply of this island is
further recognized by the rather elaborately constructed
Marie Terese Bowman Memorial Well for the public in the
center of the island. At the present time the island is
permanently inhabited by some 10 to 20 persons but
expands to several times that number at times due to
vistors.

Climate

The climate of the Belizean Barrier Reef islands
is maritime tropical. The nearest long term
climatological station is the Melinda Forest Station on
the Belizean mainland, 30 kilometers from South Water
Cay and Carrie Bow Cay. Limited climatological data has
been collected at Carrie Bow Cay. Additionally, brief
two-week periods of precipitation data were collected by
the author in May, 1988, January, 1989, and January,
1990. Figure 3 shows the distribution of rainfall for
the coastal mainland based on an isohyetal map of Belize

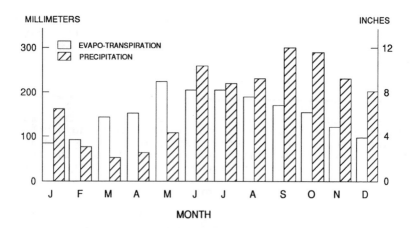

Figure 3. Plot of Mainland Precipitation and Island
Potential Evapotranspiration for Southern Belize, C.A.

by USAID (Walker, 1973). This map suggests that the islands may get as much as 80% of the mainland precipitation, which is about 2180 mm/year). Other short term records on Carrie Bow Cay (Rutzler and Mcintyre, 1982) suggest that Carrie Bow Cay gets 42% of mainland precipitation. Thus, the average annual precipitation on the islands may vary from 915 mm to 1744 mm causing a major unknown in hydrologic budget calculations. Based on observed hydrologic conditions it is believed that the higher value is more likely.

The average daily air temperature on the islands is about 27.3 C (81.1 F) with a range from a low of 24.5 C (76.1 F) in January to a high of 30 C (86 F). The temperature, combined with solar radiation is the major parameter in the calculation of potential evapotransporation. The potential evapotransporation show in Figure 3 has been calculated from a partial record of temperature and solar radiation data available for Carrie Bow Cay (Rutzler and Ferraris, 1982).

The rainfall pattern shown in Figure 2 highlights a significant dry period February through May in which the average monthly rainfall is less than one third that of the other months. The region is subject to severe tropical depressions and hurricanes which can cause short term deluges of rainfall.

Tides

In oceanic islands the dynamics of the ocean play a very important role in the viability of the fresh water lens in islands. The boundry of ocean land is ever moving both vertically and horizontally forcing the lens to constantly adjust to a new equilibrium. Within an island the lens interface between fresh water and salt water moves up and down mixing the fresh water with the salt water and creating a transition zone. Where the tidal flucuation is large, this transition zone may be considerable. The fresh water lens commonly consists of a layer of fresh water and a transistion zone of brackish to salt water. If the tidal flucuation is very large or the groundwater recharge is small there may be no fresh water in the lens at all. The smaller the island the more significant the tidal induced mixing becomes to the existance of a fresh water lens.

The tide at Carrie Bow Cay and South Water Cay is microtidal with a mean range of 15 centimeters, and is of the mixed semidiurnal type. Its' semidiurnal and diurnal amplitutes are of approximately equal importance. There can be a marked asymmetry between the

two semidiurnal   cycles during the   month.   When   tidal
components   occur simultaneously the tidal range can   be
as   great   as   50   centimeters   (Kjerfve,   1982).
Additionally,   wind   tides   and   atmosphereic   pressure
changes   can   cause   exteme   sea   level   changes.   Both
islands, but especially Carrie Bow Cay with a   land
surface of less than one meter above mean sea level, are
subject to inundation from hurricane storm surges.

Hydrogeology

        Carrie Bow Cay and South Water Cay are perched on
the   edge   of   the coastal reef flat   which   extends   24
kilometers   out   from   the   mainland.   The   islands   are
Halocene   sedimentary accumulations of   coral   fragments
and   accretions   on   pleistocene   limestone.   Leached
calcitic   limestone was subaerially exposed during   the
last   glacial period. Flooding of the bedrock occured
about 7,000 years ago. The sediments underlying the
islands   above   this   limestone   are   uncemented.   Peat,
representing former sea level stands, has been found in
sediment   cores   taken   in the lagoon near the   islands
(Shinn, et al, 1982).

        One core, RC4, located as shown on Figure 2, was
drilled to a depth of 17.7 m.   As illustrated in   the
cross-section   on Figure 4 this core   encountered

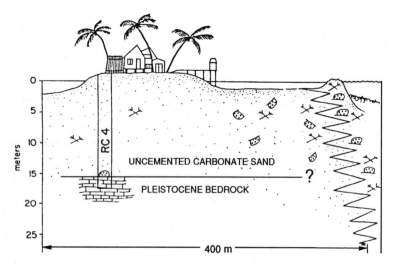

Figure 4. Geologic Section at Carrie Bow Cay , Belize.
          (after Shinn, et al, 1982)

uncemented carbonate reef sands with some coral rubble. A piece of coral obtained in the core at a depth of 15 m below present sea level gave an age of 6,960 plus or minus 110 years. The leached calcitic coralline bedrock contained root marks and iron staining indicative of subaerial exposure (Shinn, et al, 1982). Drilling has not gone deep enough to ascertain whether or not solution cavities have been formed within the limestone bedrock. In other regions of the Belizean Reef, however, submarine caves have been found. It is, therefore, quite possible that solution cavities exist which could effect the hydrogeology of the islands in a manner similar to that described by Buddemeier and Holladay, 1977, and also Wheatcraft and Buddemeier, 1981, for Pacific coral atoll islands.

Surface sediments are loose and open, allowing for substantial infiltration of precipitation. Only during the hardest rainfalls is there surface runoff.

Estimates of hydraulic conductivity were made from laboratory permeameter tests of disturbed reconstituted samples and by the tidal fluctuation analysis method described by Todd (1980). The laboratory testing gave an average value of 42 m/day for a porosity of 0.56. A most dense packing was used in the test to simulate in-situ conditions. The tidal fluctuation analysis gave a value of 46 m/day using lag time criteria and a value of 83 m/day using an attenuation criteria. It is surmised that because of the very small size of the island and the central placement of the monitor well the large value obtained from amplitute attenuation may reflect a reinforced wave; that is, the tidal wave moves through the landmass from both sides and is superimposed into a double wave effect. More field work needs to be done to support this theory.

If a value of 46 m/day is taken as an equivalent homogeneous hydraulic conductivity , KE, value for the horizontal, KH, and vertical,KV, components, and a degree of anisotrophy assumed, values can be determined for these components. Using the relationship given by Harr (1962) these components can be calculated from:

$$KE = (KH \times KV)^{0.5} \qquad\qquad (1)$$

Using an anisotrophic ratio of KH/KV equal to 10, the components of KE are KH equals 146 m/day and KV equals 14.6 m/day. For purposes of groundwater flow in the the lens, the horizontal hydraulic conductivity is the most important.

Discussion

        The thickness of the fresh water lenses at Carrie
Bow Cay and South Water Cay have been measured during
three wet seasons and during one dry season over the
period 1987-1990. Measurements have consisted of salinty
profiling extending into the fresh water-salt water
transition zone. Water samples were obtained by means of
a stainless steel small diameter probe driven to
selected depths below the water table. Representative
salinity profiles with depth for Carrie Bow Cay and
South Water Cay are shown in Figures 5 and 6.

        Wet season salinity profiles are shown in Figure
5 taken in January of 1987 approximately at the midpoint
of the widest part of each landmass. These midpoint
locations are shown in Figure 2. On tiny Carrie Bow Cay
there is a thin layer of fresh water (salinity less than
1 ppt), only a few centimeters thick, in the core of the
island. The fresh water layer rapidly becomes more

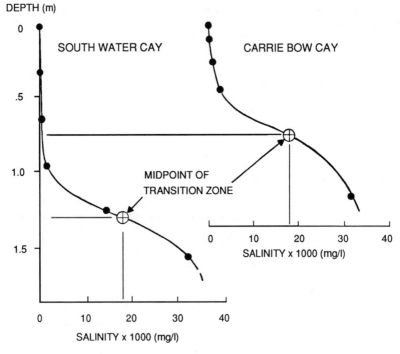

Figure 5.   Salinity Profiles on Carrie Bow Cay and South
             Water Cay during Wet Season (January, 1987).

saline nearer the shoreline and mixing from tidal action takes place. The distance from the water table to the midpoint of the transition zone, the theoretical Ghyben-Herzberg lens thickness, is approximately 0.7 m. Below this the groundwater rapidly becomes salty. On South Water Cay with a width approximately 2.6 times that of Carrie Bow Cay, the fresh water layer (salinity less than 1 ppt) extends to 0.7 m below the water table and the theoretical thickness is 1.4 m.

During the dry season, from February through May the fresh water lens shrinks. This is illustrated by two sets of salinity profiles shown in Figure 6, both taken at the midpoints of the islands. On Carrie Bow Cay the fresh water layer is completely effaced by lack of fresh water recharge during the dry season and only brackish water is found; the transition zone extends to the surface of the water table. The depth to the midpoint of the transition zone is only 0.3 m. On South Water Cay the lens shrinks from January to May but still remains

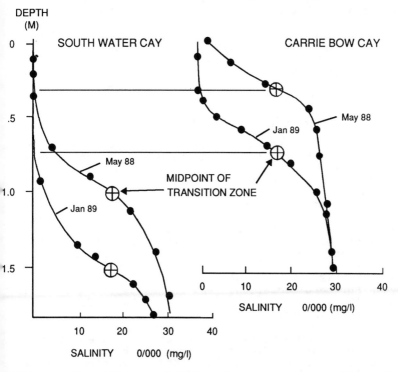

Figure 6. Comparison of Wet and Dry Season Salinity Profiles on Carrie Bow Cay and South Water Cay.

viable with a fresh water thickness of about 0.5 m and a distance to the lens midpoint of 1 m. It should be noted that though the fresh water part of the lens shrinks, the thickness of the transition zone remains relatively constant at about 1 m for both islands.

Salinity profiles at different areal locations indicates that the lens is a classical Ghyben-Herzberg lens in formation and behavior. Because of the very low diurnal tidal range of less than 0.2 m, the tidal effect is small but still measurable. If the tidal flux were much higher, it is doubtful that a fresh water layer could ever exist on Carrie Bow Cay.

The hydrogeologic model for coral islands described by Wheatcraft and Buddemeier (1981) was considered for application to Carrie Bow Cay in South Water Cay. However, while it seems possible that solution cavities may exist in the limestone bedrock underlying the unconsolidated sediments, the lens is so shallow that no abnormal vertical signal was apparent in the multi-level piezometer measurements taken.

A simple equation based on the strip island lens thickness equation by Fetter (1980) relates maximum lens size to the major controlling parameters for development of the fresh water lens namely, landmass width, permeability, relative densities of fresh and salt water, and groundwater recharge.

$$D = (W/2)(R/(ps(ps-pf)K))^{0.5} \tag{2}$$

Where D is maximum depth of lens below mean sea level, K is hydraulic conductivity, ps is salt water density, pf is fresh water density, W is width of the landmass, and R is groundwater recharge.

Inspection of Equation (2) shows that if all hydrogeologic parameters are the same, the lens thickness should vary linearly with the landmass width. The width of South Water Cay is approximately 2.6 times that of Carrie Bow Cay and the lens thickness is about 2 to 3 times that of Carrie Bow Cay. This demonstrates at least in this limited case, the validity of the simple Ghyben-Herzberg equation, and the assumption that the hydrogeologic characteristics of the islands are essentially the same.

The known parts of Equation (2) are landmass width, groundwater densities, and lens thicknesses at the center of each island. This equation can be rearranged as follows to provide a relationship for the remaining unknowns, namely recharge, R, and hydraulic conductivity, K, as a ratio.

$$(ps(ps-pf))(2D/W)^2 = R/K \qquad (3)$$

Using field measured values for yearly average lens thicknesses for each island gives a value of R/K = 0.0000150 for Carrie Bow Cay and a value of 0.0000152 for South Water Cay. This ratio can be used in conjunction with an estimated hydraulic conductivity value to calculate estimated groundwater recharge. Using an estimated horizontal hydraulic conductivity value of 146 m/day, the estimated recharge is 0.80 m/year. This seems reasonable in comparison with an estimated annual precipitation in the range of 1.7 m/year.

Summary

It is found that even on a very small landmass a fresh water can develop if conditions are favorable, namely, high of groundwater recharge, small tidal fluctuation and moderate hydraulic conductivity. Except for a relatively high hydraulic conductivity, these conditions are found on tiny Carrie Bow Cay. Thus, Carrie Bow Cay may represent an example of limiting conditions for the establishment of a fresh water lens. The investigation further shows the response of a fresh water lens to even limited dry periods of low recharge.

Comparison of the lens on Carrie Bow Cay with that found on South Water Cay enables the validity of the basic fresh water lens equation to be examined. It is found that with an assumption of similar hydrogeologic and climatic conditions on both islands, the lens size is directly proportional to island width. The relatively constant thickness of the transition zone on both islands provides evidence of similar hydrogeologic and climatic conditions. With an assumption of consistent hydrogeologic and climatic conditions a ratio of recharge to hydraulic conductivity, R/K, can be determined which should be applicable to similar reef islands.

Acknowledgement

This study was supported by the Smithsonian Institution and by the Exxon Corporation, and is Contribution Number 318 to the Caribbean Coral Reef Ecosystems Program of the Smithsonian Institution.

References

Buddemeier, R. W. and G. Holladay, 1977, "Atoll Hydrology: Island Groundwater Characteristicsand their Relationship to Diageneses", Proceedings, Third International Coral Reef Symposium, University of Miami, Miami, FL, pp.167-173.

Fetter, C. W., 1988, APPLIED HYDROGEOLOGY, 2nd Ed. Merrill Publishing Co., Columbus, Ohio, pp. 154-156.

Harr, M.E., 1962, GROUNDWATER AND SEEPAGE, McGraw Hill Book Company, New York, NY, pp. 29-31.

Kjerfve, B.,K. Rutzler and G. H. Kierspe, 1982, "Tides at Carrie Bow Cay,Belize",in The Atlantic Barrier Reef Ecosystem at Carrie Bow Cay, Belize, Smithsonian Institution Press, Washington, D. C., pp. 47-51.

Rutzler, K.and J. D. Ferrasis, 1982, "Terrestial Environment and Climate, Carrie Bow Cay, Belize", in the Atlantic Barrier Reef Ecosystem at Carrie Bow Cay, Belize, Smithsonian Institution Press, Washington, D.C., pp. 77-91.

Rutzler, K. and I.G. Macintyre, 1982, "The Habitat Distribution and Community Structure of the Barrier Reef Complex at Carrie Bow Cay, Belize", in the Atlantic Barrier Reef Ecosystem at Carrie Bow Cay, Belize, Smithsonian Institution Press, Washington, D.C. pp.9-45.

Shinn, E.A., J.H. Hudson, R.B. Haley, B. Lidz, D.M. Robin, and I.G. Macintyre, 1982, "Geology and Sediment Accumulations Rates at Carrie Bow Cay, Belize", in the Atlantic Barrier Reef Ecosystem at Carrie Bow Cay, Belize, Smithsonian Institution Press, Washington, D.C. pp. 63-75.

Stoddart, D.R., F.R. Fosberg and D.L. Spellman, 1982, "Cays of the Belize Barrier Reef and Lagoon", Atoll Research Bulletin 256, the Smithsonian Institution, Washington, D.C. pp. 18-21.

Todd, E.K., 1980, GROUNDWATER HYDROLOGY, 2nd Ed., John Wiley and Sons, New York, NY, pp. 242-245.

Walker, S.H., 1973, Map from Summary of Climatic Record for Belize, Supplement No. 3, Land Resources Division, Surbiton, Surrey, England.

Wheatcraft, S.W. and R.W. Buddemeier, 1981, "Atoll Island Hydrology", Groundwater Vol.19, No.3, pp.311-320.

THE INTERNATIONAL NORTH SEA CONFERENCES: A NEW FORCE IN MARINE REGIONAL ENVIRONMENTAL CO-OPERATION

by

David Freestone *

ABSTRACT

Despite the large number of international and regional bodies concerned with the the North Sea environment, problems persist. Existing institutions, eg the Paris and Oslo Commissions (OSPARCOM), the European Community, the Wadden Sea Secretariat, the Rhine Commission, the IMO, do not appear to be able to generate the holistic approach and political impetus to address the problems. It was to provide such an overview that the first International Conference for the Protection of the North Sea was held in Bremen in 1984; since then further meetings have been held in London in November 1987 and in The Hague in March 1990. This paper will assess the institutional significance of the International North Sea Conferences (INSCs) and their substantive contribution to international environmental co-operation.

The North Sea has been described as 'a regional sea with possibly the densest population and industrial hinterland and the greatest riverine input and seagoing traffic of any sea area in the world.' (Reid, 1990) The last decade has seen a dramatic growth in the number of indicators of environmental damage including oil spills, algal blooms, eutrophication, radical reductions in fish takes and cetacean deaths. As a semi-enclosed sea, there are no areas beyond the national jurisdiction of the littoral states, but despite the fact that the North Sea states were in the 1960s among the pioneers of seabed delimitation, the claims of the littoral states have not been upgraded as

---

* Institute of Estuarine and Coastal Studies, and Senior Lecturer in Law, University of Hull, England. Managing Editor, International Journal of Estuarine and Coastal Law, Graham and Trotman/Martinus Nijhoff, London/Dordrecht.

permitted by the 1982 LOSC (and now by customary
international law) to full Exclusive Eonomic Zone (EEZ)
claims. The concept of the EEZ permits extended
pollution control jurisdiction (see Article 55 LOSC) ,
but only France and Norway have to date established EEZs
in the North Sea. The Dutch Government is currently
pressing for the remaining North Sea states to make a
co-ordinated move to establish EEZs, but until this is
done international law imposes limits on the extent of
unilateral national jurisdiction over marine pollution
outside the territorial sea (IJlstra and Ymkers, 1989).
A variety of regional and international institutions are
addressing these issues in one way or another, but none
seems as yet abe to generate a truly holistic approach.
Indeed the very variety of such institutions itself
presents a problem of co-ordination.

Existing Institutions
Of the eight states bordering the North Sea, six (UK,
France, Belgium, Netherlands, Germany and Denmark) are
members of the European Community (EC), only Norway and
Sweden are not. The EC has established competence in
fishery regulation and the 1986 Single European Act has
provided a clear legal basis for environmental
legislation, and thus it is argued for marine
environmental protection (Prat, 1990). Regional
institutions already exist in the Commissions of the
1971 Oslo Convention on the prevention of marine
pollution by dumping from ships and aircraft (OSCOM) and
the 1974 Paris Convention for the prevention of marine
pollution from land-based sources (PARCOM), (see further
Hayward, 1990). Denmark, the Netherlands and Germany
also collaborate in measures to protect the shallow
Wadden sea off their coasts, an area which has been
described as an indicator of the health of the North Sea
as a whole. In 1982 the three countries issued a Joint
Declaration which agreed, inter alia, to establish a
Joint Secretariat (van der Zwiep, 1990). Collaboration
to improve the quality of the Rhine, a major discharger
of pollutants into the North Sea, through the Rhine
Action Programme adopted in 1987 (Nollkaemper, 1990)
also has a direct effect on the quality of the North
Sea, as does the international rQgime governing
pollution of the seas under MARPOL 1973/78, compliance
with which as well as with other international marine
treaties is also monitored and enforced on a regional
basis under the terms of the 1980 Paris Memorandum of
Understanding to which all the North Sea states are
signatory. (Kasoulides, 1990)
To this can be added regional arrangements on co-
operation in dealing with pollution of the North Sea by
oil and other dangerous substances, under the 1983 Bonn

Convention, including the understanding on air-borne surveillance of 1987; industry agreements on liability for offshore pollution (OPOL, 1974) and numerous bilateral agreements (for the texts of the instruments mentioned above, see Freestone and IJlstra 1991).

The International North Sea Conferences

Despite (some even say because of) this large number of arrangements and institutions there have been signs of further deterioration in the quality of the North Sea environment (see Peet, 1986; ten Hallers and Bijlsma, 1989). It was specifically to provide an holistic view of the problems facing the North Sea, and to provide political impetus for initiatives to improve the situation that in 1984 in Bremen the West German Government convened a meeting of Ministers from the coastal states of the North Sea concerned with protection of the North Sea. The Bremen Declaration (for text of this and the two later Declarations, see Freestone and IJlstra, 1991) provided a political basis for a common commitment to improving the environment of the North Sea and has now been developed further in Ministerial meetings in London in November 1987 and in The Hague in March 1990. These Interministerial meetings have now assumed an important dynamic of their own. Scheduled to meet again in 1995 in Denmark with an interim Ministerial Meeting in 1992, they have also sponsored the formal establishment (in December 1988) of the North Sea Task force as a scientific support group and research co-operation body to produce, inter alia, a Quality Status Report on the North Sea for 1993. (Reid, 1990). The Ministers have also agreed to participate actively in the Oslo and Paris Commission Meetings scheduled to be held in France in 1992 and to provide continuity officials will meet as regularly as possible in the interim.

The Legal Status of the INSC Meetings and their Declarations

It is a significant reflection of the level of political concern about the North Sea environment that although these Ministerial level meetings do not spring from any institutional obligation to meet - they are still in that sense ad hoc - they have nevertheless now assumed a regular pattern. Indeed it now being argued in some quarters that a North Sea Treaty should be drawn up formalising and institutionalising these new arrangements into more traditional international form (Ehlers, 1990). However there is evidence that functioning at a political level provides a degree of flexibility and occasionally a willingness to go further

down the road which a formal legal approach might well
inhibit.

The essentially ad hoc, political nature of the meetings
has also prompted debate about the legal status of the
Declarations which have become a hallmark of these
meetings. The 1984 Bremen Meeting issued a Ministerial
Declaration (known now as the Bremen Declaration) and
the subsequent meetings have also followed this format,
ie. the London Declaration of 1987 and The Hague
Declaration of 1990. These Declarations are not drawn up
like treaty provisions imposing strict obligations on
the participants. Indeed, the aspirational and qualified
language in which they are generally couched - under
which the participating states variously agree to
programmes of pollution reduction and environmental
improvement - suggests that the parties intended
political rather than legal obligation (this certainly
appears to be the interpretation taken by the UK).
Nevertheless declarations of this kind are not totally
without significance under international law. Although
they may not be intended to impose strict legal
obligations, they may however be said to impose general
obligations under international law to implement in good
faith, and parties have to that extent agreed not to
take actions which would undermine the agreed principles
and objectives. It has been suggested that the principle
of estoppel might also be invoked to release fellow
signatories from their obligations should there be an
obvious and deliberate violation of such principles or
objectives (van der Mensbrugghe, 1990).

The 1990 Hague Meeting
Space does not permit a detailed assessment of all the
issues covered by the three Declarations but a clearer
view of the nature of INS Conferences can perhaps be
derived from a brief survey of the principles endorsed
by the most recent Meeting at The Hague in March 1990
and the matters on which decisions which announced by
the final declaration.

The Hague Meeting had before it reports on the
implementation of the objectives of the 1987 London
Declaration as well as an interim Quality Status of the
North Sea Report prepared by the Task Force (which is
working to 1993 for its full Report). Despite
reservations expressed publicly by certain participants
(including the Dutch Minister who chaired the Meeting)
about implementation by the UK, the meeting as a whole
welcomed the progress reported. It also adopted (in some
cases reiterated) the following principles for its
future work:

- Improvement of control and enforcement (at national and international levels) of emission reduction regulations affecting the North Sea;

- Continued application of the Precautionary Principle. This important principle establishes that the Participants will "take action to avoid potentially damaging impacts of substances that are persistent, toxic and liable to biaccumulate even where there is no scientific evidence to prove a causal link between emissions and effects;

- Acceptance of the concepts of sustained use and sustainable development, as well as the integrated ecosystem approach indicated by the World Commission on Environment and Development (the Bruntland Report);

- Acceptance of the following as the basis for pollution reduction in the North Sea:

- further development of non/low waste processes and environmentally non-hazardous products;

  - integrated approach to environmental management of anthropogenic sources of land-based pollution from riverine and atmospheric sources;
  - co-operation with industry to reduce polluting emissions at source by BAT (best available technology). Note that the definition of BAT adopted by the INSCs takes into account "economic availability".
  - further reduction of environmentally threatening accident risks, and improvement of accident response procedures, etc;
  - continued combination of advantages of approaches based on environmental quality objectives and emission standards.

The Hague Declaration
The main issues agreed by the Hague Meeting were set out in the Declaration under the following heads:

Inputs of Hazardous Substances
The 1987 London Declaration had agreed to aim at the achievement between 1985 and 1995 of "a substantial reduction in the order of 50%" of inputs to the North Sea of hazardous substances, (ie. those which are "persistent, toxic and liable to bioaccumulate"). In continuation of these policies the Meeting agreed to measures to further reduce all such inputs (whether anthropogenic or

not). New targets of up to 70% reductions were
clarified.

Phasing out of PCBs

The environmental threat posed by PCBs was
considered to be so severe that to prevent PCBs and
hazardous PCB-substitutes from entering the marine
environment Participating States agreed to take
measures to phase out and to aim to destroy
completely, in an environmentally safe manner, all
identifiable PCBs "as soon as possible". Co-
operation in the development of safe destruction
techniques as well as safe PCB-substitutes, and
future control of PCBs would be pursued through a
range of regional (ie OSPARCOM and EEC) and
international bodies.

Inputs of Nutrients

The reduction of nutrient inputs - thought to be
the cause of eutrophication in areas of the North
Sea - provides a useful example of the
precautionary principle. A programme of reduction
is already established by the Paris Commission, but
in addition the North Sea States agreed to identify
actual "eutrophication problem areas" in the North
Sea as well as potential problem areas. They agreed
that for the North Sea catchment area all sewage
from urban areas and equivalent industries should
receive secondary (biological) treatment, unless
exempted on a case-by-case basis.

Dumping and Incineration at Sea

Sewage Sludge and Industrial Waste Dumping

The London Declaration had included an undertaking
in principle to end dumping of polluting materials
in the North Sea at the "earliest practicable"
date. The UK is still a major North Sea dumper -
half of all industrial waste dumped there comes
from the UK, as well as an appreciable proportion
of dredging spoil. The UK is the only state to dump
sewage sludge. The exact extent of the London
Declaration undertakings are not clear - not only
are the provisions loosely drafted, but they also
appear to be internally contradictory. Nevertheless
dumping by the UK is a major political issue
roundly condemned by other North Sea states. The UK
Minister for the Environment attempted to defuse
this issue by announcing a few days before the
Hague Meeting that the UK would end Sewage Dumping
by the end of 1998 and Industrial Waste Dumping as
soon as possible and no later than the end of 1992
(with an extension into 1993 only if "absolutely
necessary").

Dumping of Dredged Material
Improvement of the quality of dredging spoil
relates directly to control of emissions of
contaminants, which find their way into the spoil.
The Oslo Commission has an established programme in
this area - which the Meeting undertook to apply.

Incineration at Sea
The London Meeting had agreed to phase out
incineration at sea by the end of 1994. The Hague
Meeting brought this target forward to the end of
1991, and agreed to seek a legal agreement under
the Oslo Convention to this effect by the end of
1990.

Pollution from Ships
Regimes for control of pollution from ships already
exist under MARPOL 1973/78. At a special meeting of
the IMO Marine Environmental Protection Committee
in October 1989 the North Sea was declared a
Special Area for the purposes of Annex V of MARPOL
(which relates to garbage) in accordance with the
decision of the 1987 London INSC. The additional
proposal, pressed vigorously by the FRG at the
Hague, for collective agreement to designate the
North Sea as a Special Area for the purposes of
Annex I (relating to discharges of oil) and II
(other hazardous substances) has been temporarily
shelved in view of the commitment of Participants
to "take concerted action" within IMO to make the
discharge requirements of both Annexes more strict
globally. However, the German proposal of Special
Area status has been held over to 1993 for
consideration at the ministerial working group, and
may be revived if inadequate progress is made at
IMO. Further measures were also agreed to be taken
through IMO, and under the Paris MOU.

Pollution from Offshore Installations
Measures to reduce pollution from operational
discharges from offshore installations a series of
measures, mostly through the Paris Commission were
agreed, including the strict regulation, and
eventual elimination, of the discharge of
contaminated cuttings.

Discharges and Disposal of Radioactive Waste
The participants agreed to continue to use BAT to
reduce radioactive discharges in association with
the competent international organisations. However,
the UK unilaterally refused to accept a further
declaration that "the North Sea is not suitable for

the dumping of radioactive waste nor for disposal of such waste into the seabed." Although this decision was stated to be made "in accordance with the recommendations of the competent International Organisation", the UK, while making it clear that it had no present intention to make any such disposals, argued that the competent international authorities had not actually declared this method of disposal unsuitable.

Airborne Surveillance

This has been a preoccupation of all three INSCs. The Meeting undertook to improve its effectiveness and to encourage the Contracting Parties to the 1983 Bonn Agreement (on Co-operation in dealing with Pollution of the North Sea by Oil and other Harmful Substances) to continue to develop remote sensing techniques for identification of pollution.

The Wadden Sea

The three Wadden Sea States produced their own recommendations contained in a Statement annexed to the Declaration, which the Meeting noted, and agreed to implement where appropriate.

Enhancement of Scientific Knowledge

The North Sea Task Force, which for the first time has attempted to gather systematically scientific data on the North Sea and to ensure co-ordination between research, modelling and monitoring programmes in the riparian states, had made reports on two matters which had attracted a great deal of public attention: algal blooms and the epidemic seal deaths. As a follow up, it was asked to continue its assessment of research on these problems as well as to extend its existing biological monitoring programme. It was also asked to address five "sensitive" issues:the impact of fishing on the North Sea ecosystem;surveillance of chemicals not usually covered in routine monitoring;the environmental impact of persistent chemicals;the role of atmospheric inputs as a source of contaminants in the North Sea; and assessment of existing damage.

Coastal State Jurisdiction

The Netherlands was invited to "initiate the co-ordination of such action and to submit the findings to North Sea Ministers by the beginning of 1992."

Salvage of Sunken Ships and/or Hazardous Cargoes
> Participants supported the early entry into force of the IMO 1989 Salvage Convention, and agreed to support IMO in its preparations for a Convention on Hazardous and Noxious Substances; they also agreed to take action through IMO to ensure sufficient salvage capacity worldwide. The EC Commission was asked to co-ordinate investigations of means of rendering harmless ships and cargoes sunken in the North Sea.

Protection of Habitats and Species
> It was agreed to "give further protection to marine wildlife in the North Sea and to tackle important gaps in knowledge which remain". A number of detailed actions to achieve these goals were agreed. North Sea states not parties to the 1979 Bonn Convention on the conservation of migratory species of wild animals were urged to join (ie Belgium and France). A Memorandum of understanding on the protection of small cetaceans in the North Sea was annexed to the Declaration, and the participants welcomed progress on a regional agreement on small cetaceans under the auspices of the Bonn Convention.

Fisheries
> The charge given to the Task Force of considering the impact of fisheries on the North Sea ecosystem was the reflection of this substantive issue on the agenda, also recorded in the Declaration. Given the socio-economic importance of fisheries, it was agreed to consider further both the impact of fisheries on the ecosystem as well as the impact of the marine environment on fisheries. Participants agreed to continue efforts in this direction - as well as to ensure satisfactory levels of fish stocks. Although not all participants (notably Norway) are EC Members, nevertheless such action will inevitably have to be taken through the EC Common Fisheries Policy.

Conclusions

The North Sea provides a particularly vivid example of the problems of co-ordination and lack of overview which result from a proliferation of regional and functional organisations and arrangements. The INSCs seek to provide that holistic view, but without replacing it with a new organisation with jurisdictional and competence problems of its own. There is no international secretariat, the majority of INSC agreements relate to future action to be taken through existing more formal organisations, such as the EC, the

Oslo and Paris Commissions or even IMO. Their very existence represents a disturbing recognition at the highest levels of the seriousness of the environmental problems facing the North Sea which existing institutions are not solving. It is this challenge which has led to the emergence of new approaches, such as that of the precautionary principle which finds important recognition in the Declarations and in the implementing actions of the functional bodies (see PARCOM Recommendation 89/1 on the use of this principle).

This paper has sought to show that the INSCs provide an important model for regional environmental co-operation which may be of considerable relevance even to those from other regions.

REFERENCES

P. Ehlers, 'The History ofthe International North Sea Conferences' in Freestone and IJlstra (1990) 3-14.

D. Freestone and T. IJlstra, (eds) **The North Sea: Perspectives on Regional Environmental Co-operation,** Graham and Trotman/Martinus Nijhoff, London/Dordrecht, 1990

D. Freestone and T. IJlstra, (eds) **The North Sea: Basic Legal Documents on Regional Environmental Co-operation,** Graham and Trotman/Martinus Nijhoff, London/Dordrecht, 1991.

P. Hayward, 'The Oslo and Paris Commissions' in Freestone and IJlstra (1990) 91-100.

T. IJlstra, 'Regional Co-operation in the North Sea: An Inquiry', (1988) 3 **International Journal of Estuarine and Coastal Law** 181-207.

T. IJlstra and P. Ymkers, 'The Netherlands and the Establishment of the Exclusive Economic Zone (1989) 4 **International Journal of Estuarine and Coastal Law** 224-229.

A. Nollkaemper, 'The Rhine Action Programme: A turning point in the protection of the North Sea ?'in Freestone and IJlstra (1990) 123-138.

G. Peet, (ed) **Reasons for Concern: the status ofthe North Sea environment,** Workgroep Noordzee, Amsterdam, 1986.

J.-L. Prat, 'The Role of the European Communities in the protection and the preservation of the marine

environment of the North Sea' in Freestone and IJlstra (1990) 101-110.

C. Reid, 'The work of the North Sea Task Force' in Freestone and IJlstra (1990) 80-88.

C. ten Hallers-Tjabbes and A. Bijlsma, (eds) **Distress Signals: signals from the environment in policy and decision-making,** Workgroep Noordzee, Amsterdam, 1989.

Y. van der Mensbrugghe,'The legal status of International North Sea Conference Declarations' in Freestone and IJlstra (1990) 15-22.

K. van der Zweip, 'The Wadden Sea: A yardstick for a clean North Sea' in Freestone and IJlstra (1990) 201-214.

TROPICAL CARBONATE COASTAL PROCESSES

John A. Black[1]

ABSTRACT

One of the most distinctive feature of tropical and subtropical carbonate coasts is their tendency to lithify to form beach rock and eolianite. Once formed, the beach rock and eolianite is more easily eroded by chemical and physical processes than is volcanic rock.

Since these coastlines shift rather rapidly from their unconsolidated to their consolidated, and back once again to their unconsolidated forms, the amount of sediment supplied to the longshore transport system is extremely variable. As a result, coastal processes change more rapidly in these areas than along the coastlines of more northerly and southerly latitudes.

INTRODUCTION

The carbonate coasts of the tropics and subtropics are remarkable for the rapid cycling of calcium carbonate from its dissolved to its solid and, once again to its dissolved form. In its solid form the calcium carbonate may be present as unconsolidated materials ranging from boulders to silt and clay-sized particles. Alternatively, it may be present as consolidated rock.

Much of the carbonate composing these coastal areas originates as hydrogenous sediment precipitated from seawater as sand-sized particles. These sediments may

[1]Suffolk Community College, Selden, New York 11784, U.S.A.

lithify to form beach rock and eolianite. Mechanical weathering in the supralittoral, the littoral and in the nearshore environment reconverts these rock types to unconsolidated materials, while chemical weathering of lithified dunes located above the supralittoral may redissolve the eolianite. The dissolved carbonates may then enter the marine environment by stream flow or, more commonly, dissolved in groundwater.

Thus, rapid shifts in the rate of sediment supplied to the longshore current are common along the carbonate coasts of the tropics and subtropics. Such shifts in sediment supply exert profound effects on tropical and subtropical coastal processes.

CARIBBEAN COASTAL FEATURES

Many Caribbean coastlines are composed primarily of calcium carbonate. The carbonates may be lithified and present as beach rock, eolianite and relict coral reefs, or may be present as unconsolidated sediments ranging in size from boulders to silt and clay-sized particles. The sand, silt and clay-sized particles may originate from the direct precipitation of calcium carbonate from seawater. Alternatively, these sediments, like the boulders, cobbles and pebbles, may be derived from the weathering of beach rock, eolianite and reef materials.

Perhaps the most distinctive feature of these coastlines is their tendency to lithify rather rapidly to form beach rock and eolianite. The beach rock lithifies subaerially to form long pavements whose width roughly corresponds to that of the littoral zone in which it was formed. Eolianite forms landward of the supralittoral zone while living reefs are commonly found seaward of the littoral zone in the near shore environment.

Along emergent coasts, however, these rock types are found well inland where the eolianite and beach rock indicate previous coastal areas and the relict reef marks former offshore environments. Along submergent or erosional coasts the eolianite may be found in the littoral zone or further offshore while the beach rock, indicating the former littoral zone, is found seaward of the eolianite.

It is also common to find eolianite formed above relict reefs. This occurs when a coral reef, through tectonic or eustatic sealevel changes, becomes raised to or above the littoral zone. The relict reef then serves to trap wind-blown sands to form an unconsolidated dune that can ultimately lithify. The beach rock along such emergent coasts is found seaward of the eolianite-relict reef complex in the supralittoral or further inland depending upon the extent of emergence.

Along erosional or submergent coastlines, however, tectonic, eustatic or erosional events may place the eolianite in the littoral zone or the near shore environment. The beach rock in these areas will be found offshore of the eolianite. In the littoral zone these rock types provide suitable substrate for intertidal organisms. When placed further offshore the eolianite and beach rock may provide suitable substrate for coral which may be found above the beach rock and/or eolianite.

MECHANISMS OF LITHIFICATION

The lithification of calcium carbonate and the geomorphology of limestone and karst has been discussed by Trudgill (1985) and Jennings (1985). The formation of beach rock and eolianite, though less well known, has been summarized by Kaye (1959), and more recently by Black (1989, 1990). In all cases lithification involves cementation by aragonite and calcite.

The calcium carbonate involved in the formation of beach rock originates from one or a combination of several sources. It may be precipitated directly from seawater when the saturation point of calcium carbonate is exceeded. It may also be carried into the littoral zone dissolved in acidic river or groundwater and then precipitate in the more basic coastal waters. Alternatively, the calcium carbonate may be precipitated on falling tides when the littoral zone is exposed to the atmosphere and the interstitial water evaporates. Precipitation may also occur in the littoral zone when the dissolved calcium carbonate, carried to the coastal environment by surface fresh water sources, mixes with and raises the total carbonate concentration of the sea/fresh water above its saturation point. In addition, Cloud (1952) and Emery, et al (1948) hold that cementation may be biochemically induced through the mediation of the cyanobacteria.

Eolianite is formed by the lithification of unconsolidated dunes composed of calcium carbonate. Unconsolidated dunes are commonly formed by the eolian transport of sediments from the littoral and supralittoral zones. Once formed, xerophilic vegetation will begin to occupy the unconsolidated dune. Metabolic processes occuring in the root zone will release carbon dioxide which, during periods of rainfall, will convert to carbonic acid, thereby decreasing pH of the water percolating through the dune. The decrease in pH facilitates the dissolution of the calcium carbonate composing the dune. The disolved calcium carbonate is then reprecipitated to form eolianite as the dune dries and the water is evaporated and/or transpired.

Recent field work on Cat Island, Bahamas and Jamaica, W.I. may have revealed three additional mechanisms of lithification. These mechanisms involve: 1) the formation of carbonate rock in tide pools, 2) in the notches of raised rock and cliff faces and 3) as a thin veneer of fine grained rock over coarser grained rock in the littoral and supralittoral zones or as descrete fine-grained rock in the littoral zone.

The lithification of calcium carbonate in tide pools occurs in the high littoral zone or in the supralittoral where flooding by seawater is infrequent. In such areas the seawater will tend to evaporate prior to the next flooding. As the water evaporates the saturation point of calcium carbonate is exceeded and the carbonate will precipitate and ultimately lithify. Such lithification leads to the filling of the tide pool. Such areas are distinguished by patches of fine grained rock, generally somewhat circular in shape, interspersed with the apparently older, coarser grained rock.

Notches above the littoral zone will accumulate sediments, shells and other debris during storm events. During periods of more moderate weather these notches are rarely flooded. Thus, the sediments deposited during storm events dry and ultimately lithify. In these cases the newly lithified sediments are found as descrete bands below the apparently older, generally coarser grained rock.

The third mechanism involves the formation, movement, deposition and ultimate lithification of fine grained sediments in the size range of silts (4-62 microns) and clay (< 4 microns). Such lithification results in the formation of fine grained caps of uniform thickness over large sections of relict reef and eolianite in the littoral zone. Alternatively, discrete fine grained rocks are formed in the littoral zone. The carbonates that ultimately form these rocks are thought to be deposited by groundwater when it enters the littoral and supralittoral zone. These carbonates may be present in groundwater in either their particulate or dissolved form and are deposited in the littoral and supralittoral zones when the groundwater intersects the land's surface and disperses.

The dissolved carbonate present in groundwater most likely originates from inland sources. Since the coastal plain of many Caribbean islands are composed primarily of carbonate, rain falling on the uplands will readily percolate through the sediments, dissolve carbonate and enter the aquifer. The dissolved carbonate will move with the groundwater and be precipitated when this water mixes with the more basic seawater in the littoral zone or when the groundwater surfaces and evaporates in the supralittoral zone.

The particulate carbonate may be either carried down into the aquifer during periods of rainfall or originate as sediments present in the beds of subaerial streams which are placed in suspension during periods of high velocity stream flow. Regardless of the origin of the particulates, the groundwater in which they are transported could be expected to be at or near its saturation point in terms of dissolved calcium carbonate. Thus, these sediments would not tend to dissolve. Rather, the very fine silt and clay-sized sediments would travel with the groundwater to be discharged where the aquifer intersects the land's surface, either in the littoral or supralittoral zones. These very fine sediments would then tend to cover the surfaces of the adjacent rock. The groundwater that enters the littoral or supralittoral would disperse, while the suspended materials will settle to form very fine grained rock in the littoral zone.

In both cases these sediments will eventually lithify as the interstitial water evaporates. The lithified "clay" covering the rock will form a solid cap of uniform thickness above the older eolianite or reef rock. The sediments that lithify in the littoral zone will form descrete fine grained rock marking the points of entry of groundwater into the coastal zone.

EFFECTS OF LITHIFICATION ON SEDIMENT TRANSPORT

Since carbonate sediments lithify rather rapidly the rate of sediment supplied to the longshore transport system is variable. As a result, sediment budgets along tropical and subtropical carbonate coasts may undergo profound changes in a relatively short time frame. Such alterations in sediment supply are profoundly affected by the wave energy expended upon a particular coastline as well as tectonic and eustatic events that have or are occurring. These changes may be localized and confined to the immediate area, may be reflected on beaches downcurrent, or may alter the geomorphology of large portions of a coastline.

Localized effects involve the armoring of the shoreline immediately landward of the lithified area.

Such armoring, however, will generally reduce the sediment supplied to the longshore current which results in a recession of downcurrent beaches. Large scale effects involve the alteration of the waves approaching a given coastline as they encounter offshore eolianite. Depending upon the energy regime of the approaching waves, the coastline may recede significantly to assume an arcuate form or accrete and may eventually reattach the offshore eolianite to the mainland.

Although beach rock forms subaerially it frequently becomes exposed in the littoral zone along localized sections of a given coastline. Should the beachface landward of such a lithified littoral zone be composed of unconsolidated material it will be protected during periods when low to moderate energy waves strike the coast. The consolidated littoral zone will, however, supply little, if any sediment to the supralittoral. As a result, the supralittoral will build at a lesser rate than it would were the littoral zone composed of unconsolidated materials. A reduction in the rate of sediment accumulation in the supralittoral may reduce the rate of dune formation. During storm events sediment will be removed from the supralittoral at a greater rate causing a recession of this area and further hindering beach and dune formation landward of the lithified littoral. Moreover, a lithified littoral zone will supply sediment at a lower rate to the longshore current. Thus, the sediment supply to downcurrent beaches will be reduced and these areas may experience a chronic recession (Black, 1990).

Lithified dunes provide significant protection to landward areas. Unlike unconsolidated dunes, however, eolianite provides little, if any, sediment to unconsolidated beaches immediately seaward. Thus, these beaches may recede during storm events. Eolianite found in the littoral zone of sumbergent or erosional coasts will reduce the sediment supplied to the longshore current and this reduction may be reflected in a recession of the down current beaches. Relict reefs raised to or above the littoral zone by tectonic or eustatic events will have much the same effect on coastal processes as does eolianite in similar locations (Black, 1990).

As noted, eustatic, tectonic or erosional events, may place eolianite offshore of the littoral zone. The lower portions of these dune systems may be submerged while the upper portions may be well above the high tide horizon. Such offshore eolianite may have one or two effects on large sections of a given coastline. These effects are dependant upon the characteristics of the waves approaching the coastline and determine whether a given reach will accrete or recede.

According to Kaye (1959), the propensity of a coastline to gain or lose sediment is dependant upon the heights and periods of the waves approaching a given area. Short period waves of less than eight seconds with heights greater than 1.5 meters and long period waves with heights greater than 1.8 meters will remove sediments from a coastline while long period waves with heights between 0.9 and 1.8 meters will lead to progradation of the shoreline. These conditions, summarized in Table I, are primarily dependant upon the fetch.

TABLE I

Wave Climate	Wave Period	Wave Height(m.)	Effect
A	long	0.9-1.8	accretion
B	short	>1.5	recession
C	long	>1.8	recession

Along coastlines subject to wave climate A, the submerged portions of the eolianite will dissipate energy to some extent, while the above water portions will do so even more effectively. In either case the velocity of the longshore current is reduced and the littoral and supralittoral zones immediately landward will build. Since, however, the velocity returns to normal along the reach immediately downcurrent of the offshore eolianite a recession of these beaches can be expected. Submerged and emergent relict reefs as well as living reefs, will also reduce the wave energy along such coasts and lead to a progradation of the shoreline with a similar recession along the downcurrent beaches.

Coastlines landward of offshore eolianite and raised relict reefs which are subject to wave climate B or C, will tend to lose sediment and develop an arcuate geomorphology. This occurs when sections of the offshore eolianite or raised relict reef breach and remain submerged resulting in a discontinous line of lithified dunes or raised reef.

Waves entering the near shore environment will be refracted by the bottom contours and diffracted around the above water sections of the reef or eolianite. Such refraction and diffraction will widen the original breach, focus wave energy on the coastline and remove sediment from the beach face resulting in the formation of an arcuate shoreline. Sediment loss will continue until the coastline retreats toward, and encounters, a secondary dune system, if present. As this system erodes and enters the supralittoral or littoral zone, the loss of sediment will be reduced and the shoreline will straighten. Should, however, the coastline continue to submerge or the secondary dune breach, the process will be repeated until a tertiary dune system, if present, is encountered.

In the West Indies conditions conducive to the formation of arcuate coastlines exist only on the Atlantic side of the easterly islands. These are the only coasts exposed to the long fetch necessary to form a Type B or C wave climate. The other coastlines are subject to a Type A wave climate and do not form arcuate coasts. In addition to a long fetch, a rapidly rising shoreline with few shoals is necessary to form arcuate coastlines. These conditions, in conjunction with wave climates B or C, enable waves to break directly on shore thereby removing sediment from the beach face. Kaye (1959) notes that these conditions are most common along the Atlantic coasts of the easterly islands during the winter months and are due to offshore storm generated waves.

SUMMARY

The processes that occur along the carbonate coasts of the tropics and subtropics are akin to those of the ice free coasts of more northerly or southerly latitudes. For example, rock is reduced to smaller materials by identical chemical and physical processes. The sediments that are produced are then sorted and transported, deposited and removed from a given reach by identical, predictable processes.

The major difference between tropical and subtropical carbonate coasts and those of the temperate zones, as well as igneous and metamorphic tropical and subtropical coasts, is in the rate of sediment production. Along temperate coasts of all rock types and non-carbonate tropical and subtropical coasts, there is a net production of sediment as the materials composing these coastlines weather. While carbonate coasts also weather to form sediment these sediments may lithify rather rapidly to re-form rock. Thus, along the carbonate coasts of the tropics and subtropics there may be a net loss of sediment as the carbonates lithify.

The lithification of carbonate results in rapid coastal changes both in the immediate area and along large sections of a given coastline. The formation and exposure of beach rock, while armoring the littoral zone, provides less sediment to the supralittoral immediately landward. Such a reduction in sediment supply leads to a reduced rate of dune and beach building. Moreover, since the littoral is converted to a rock substrate, less sediment is supplied to the longshore transport system and this will cause a recession of the beaches downcurrent.

Eolianite above the supralittoral will protect more landward areas. During storm events, however, lithified dunes provide less sediment to the beach face and long-shore current. As a result the beach face will tend to lose sediment at these times while the paucity of sediment supplied to the longshore current will lead to a recession of downcurrent beaches. Eolianite and relict reef in the littoral zone will have much the same effect on coastal processes as does exposed beach rock.

Offshore eolianite may cause a coastline to accrete or recede depending upon the wave climate. Accretion can be expected with wave climate A. The presence of offshore eolianite, in this case, reduces the velocity of the longshore current. As a result, less sediment is transported downcurrent. Once beyond the influence of the offshore eolianite, however, the velocity of the longshore current will return to normal. When this occurs, a recession of the beaches in this area is to be expected.

Along beaches subjected to energy climate B and C the offshore eolianite will refract and diffract the approaching waves thereby focusing energy on the coastline. This will lead to a broad-scale recession and result in the formation of cupsate coastlines and crescent shaped bays.

Since, however, carbonate rock is more easily eroded, beach rock, eolianite and relict reefs mechanically weather to form sediment in a comparatively short time frame. As a result the sediment supply will be reestablished more rapidly than along tropical and subtropical coasts composed of igneous and metamorphic rock.

ACKNOWLEDGEMENTS

Funding for this study was provided by a Faculty Development Grant from the State University of New York. I am particularly indebted to Lorry and Jack McCormick of Cat Island, Bahamas for their hospitality and logistical support and to Michele McCormick for her help and

observations in the field.   Hayden Romano and Charmaine
Delpesh of the Institute of Marine Affairs, Trinidad,
W.I. generously showed me the beaches of the north coast
of Trinidad.   Gene Kaplan, Director of the Hofstra
University Laboratory, St. Ann's Bay, Jamaica, W.I.
provided laboratory space and a base of operations while
on that island.   Wendy and Ray Van Barnveld, Resident
Director and Naturalist respectively, of the Hofstra
facility provided valuable logistical support and advice.
Appreciation is also extended to Karen Kluber for
secretarial assistance and Ray Welch for commenting on
this paper.

BIBLIOGRAPHY

Black, J.A., 1989, "Various Rocky Coastlines of the
    Tropics and Subtropics", Shore and Beach, Vol.
    57, No. 2 pp. 25-31

_____, 1990, "The Effects of Lithified Calcium
    Carbonate on Tropical Coastal Processes",
    Transactions: Geologoical Society of Trinidad
    and Tobago, Trinidad, W.I.

Cloud, P.E., 1952, Preliminary Report on the Geology and
    Marine Environments of Onotoan Atoll, Gilbert
    Islands, National Research Council, Atoll Res.
    Bul. No. 12 pp. 1-73

Emery, K.O., J.I. Tracey and H.S. Ladd, 1948. Geology of
    Bikini and Nearby Atolls, Geol. Survey Prof.
    Paper 260-A. U.S. Gov. Print. Off.,Washington,
    D.C.

Jennings, J.N., 1985, Karst Geomorphology, Basil
    Blackwell, N.Y.

Kaye, C.A., 1959, "Shoreline Features and Quarternary
    Shoreline Changes: Puerto Rico", Geol. Survey
    Prof. Paper 317-B.   U.S. Gov. Print. Off.,
    Washington, D.C.

Trudgill, S., 1985, Limestone Geomorphology, Longman,
    London

THE HYDROLOGY OF A CARIBBEAN MANGROVE ISLAND

Raymond M. Wright[1], M. ASCE
Daniel W. Urish[2], M. ASCE
Igor Runge[3], A. M. ASCE

ABSTRACT

The hydrology of an overwashed mangrove island was investigated. Various hydrologic data were used to calculate Manning's roughness factor, n, in two reaches. Results indicate n varies highly over the tidal cycle.

INTRODUCTION

In general, a mangrove ecosystem is an essential part of the typical tropical coast environment. Yet it has been severely impacted in many regions of the world from man's abuse and lack of appreciation of it's importance. Mangroves protect the coastline from the erosive forces of storm waves and promote land-building processes by trapping sediment and producing peat.

The protective structure of the subtidal root system of the red mangrove (Rhizophora) serve as the nursery for the juveniles of many deep water fish and crustaceans ranging from tarpon to lobster. Several researchers state that the mangrove may be more than 20 times as productive in support of the fish populations as the open ocean.

Though the mangrove seems to thrive in the dynamic coastal environment, it is quite sensitive to pollution. Silts and oils can be particularly damaging by coating the respiratory parts of the intertidal prop and air roots, which shut off the essential oxygen supply

---

[1] Associate Professor, Civil and Environmental Eng., University of Rhode Island, Kingston, RI 02881
[2] Chairman, Civil and Environmental Eng., University of Rhode Island, Kingston, RI 02881
[3] Assistant Professor, Civil and Environmental Eng., University of Rhode Island, Kingston, RI 02881

(Ruetzler and Feller 1988).

The mangrove island complex of Twin Cays lies some 22 km off the coast of Belize just inside of the Belizean Barrier Reef (Figure 1). It has been the site of extensive scientific study by the Smithsonian Institution since the early 1980s under the Caribbean Coral Reef Ecosystems Program (CCRE). This study is a part of that program and focuses on the dynamic hydrological system of this mangrove island complex.

BACKGROUND INFORMATION

The intertidal islands of Twin Cays, because of their isolated, undisturbed condition, provide an excellent opportunity to study a natural mangrove community. The knowledge gained from these islands are considered an ecological baseline, which enables a comparison to similar ecosystems already subject to the impact of man.

Twin Cays is composed of two main islands, East Island with an area of about 300 ha and West Island of about 200 ha. The principal component of this study provides information pertaining to the general hydrology of West Island, a kidney shaped landmass about 2000 m long and 500 m wide (Figure 2).

Substrata geological studies by the Smithsonian Institution found that sediment with evidence of mangrove growth extends 8 m below the present level of the islands to a dense limestone substrate. It is believed the mangrove ecosystem was established on a topographic high of patch reef some 7000 years ago, and the growth kept pace with rise in sea level (Ruetzler and Feller 1988). The present bottom is composed of soft, silty organic muck. Where higher levels of the intertidal bottom are exposed to the air for longer periods, a thin salt crust may form. In a few areas near the margins of the islands coral sand ridges may exist.

The islands of Twin Cays are dominated by the red mangrove (Rhizophora) and the black mangrove (Avicennia), although some buttonwood trees (Conocarpus) can be found above the intertidal zone. The flooded central intertidal region of West Island, where this study was conducted, is exclusively red mangrove. According to the classification of Lugo and Snedaker (1974), the Twin Cays ecosystem is an "overwashed mangrove island" or an island frequently overwashed by tides with a high rate of organic export.

The interior of the larger islands of Twin Cays contain large unvegetated mud flats and shallow ponds.

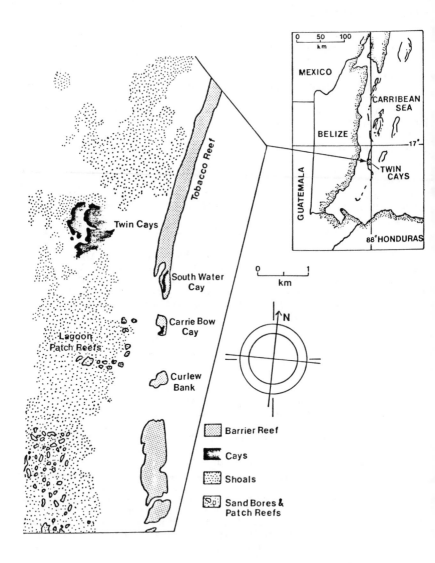

FIGURE 1. General location of Twin Cays, Belize. (Adopted from
Ruetzler and Macintyre, 1982.)

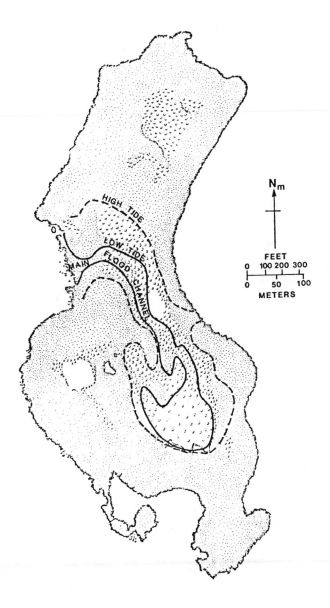

FIGURE 2. West Island; Twin Cays, Belize.

Yet numerous stumps of large trees in the mud flats attest to the fact of a more hospitable environment in the not too distant past.   These may be the type of regions Holdridge (1940) refers to as "salitrals", a result of hypersalination.   Also, around the margins of these dead areas are severely stunted widely spaced red mangroves.   While it appears these areas are the victim of severe environmental stress, the stress mechanism is not clear.   A better understanding of the hydrologic system with its associated knowledge of tidal flooding and flushing, salinity and temperature variations, and nutrient transport may provide a more specific answer.

The highest parts of the islands of Twin Cays are less than 1 m above mean sea level with much of the central part below mean sea level.   During storm events complete inundation of the mangrove island is likely.

The nearest long term climatological station is at the Melinda Forest Station on the Belizean mainland, some 30 km distance from Twin Cays.   Limited climatological information has also been collected at Carrie Bow Cay, a small Island 3 km to the southeast from Twin Cay. Additionally, brief two week periods of precipitation data were collected by the authors in May, 1988, January 1989 and January 1990.

The long term record for the mainland station is shown in Figure 3.   The pattern for Twin Cays is believed to be similar, but somewhat less in magnitude.   Ruetzler and Macintyre (1982) estimated the precipitation on Carrie Bow Cay as 42% of the mainland precipitation based on a partial four year record.   Extrapolation of an isohyetal map for Belize by USAID based on all available data indicates that Twin Cays may cet as much as 80% of the mainland precipitation.   The rainfall pattern highlights a pronounced dry period February through May in which the average monthly rainfall is less than one third that of the other months.

The seasonal climatic variation have a profound effect on the monthly hydrologic budget, particularly during May when rainfall is low and the high temperature causes high evapotranspiration losses in the island interior.   The approximate seasonal relationships of precipitation, temperature and evapotranspiration based on the limited available information is also shown in Figure 3.   The average air temperature is about 27.3°C (81.1°F) with a range from a low of 24.5°C (76.1°F) in January to a high of 30°C (86°F) in May.   The potential evapotranspiration has been calculated from a partial record of temperature and solar radiation data available for Carrie Bow Cay (Ruetzler and Macintyre 1982).   A

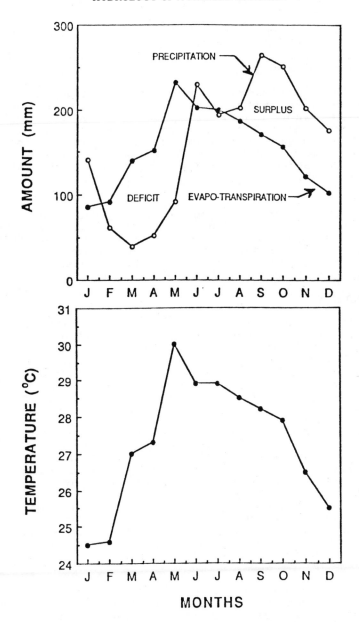

FIGURE 3. Annual precipitation (top) and air temperature (bottom) record for the Twin Cays region.

simple water budget analysis for West Pond shows that a monthly water deficit, with no runoff, exists for February through May, and that an excess exists during June through January.

With respect to tides even a a small range may cause major changes in the environmental relationship of mangrove, land and water. The tide in the lagoon surrounding Twin Cays is microtidal and of the mixed semidiurnal type. The extent of flooding on West Island due to a mean tidal range of 15 cm is also shown in Figure 2. Because of the flat topography of the island the area flooded may easily double during one tidal cycle.

Past research at the nearby island, Carrie Bow Cay, has shown that if the high water for the tidal components occur simultaneously, the maximum tide range could be as much as 50 cm. Also, wind and storm enhanced tides can cause extreme sea level changes even greater than the astronomical forces (Kjerfve, et al. 1982).

METHODOLOGY

The data necessary to characterize the hydrology of West Island was obtained by a variety of methods. These included field transit surveys, automated water level data collection, water quality sampling, dye studies, flow measurements and low level balloon photography. In order to determine the effect of seasonal variations, field work was done near the end of the wet season in January and also near the end of the dry season in June.

Topography and hydrography were determined for the tidal flood region extending from open water at the West Bay Lagoon along the channel to West Pond. Some 36 semipermanent reference points were established to locate water level and water quality measurements. These consisted of PVC pipes driven into the ground. Horizontal control was determined by tape and surveying transit measurements. Vertical control was established for the top of the pipes by leveling to an arbitrary datum established at the Twin Cay dock bench mark. The elevation assigned to this bench mark was 3.05 m (10.00 ft).

The two principle surveying transects included: (1) from the lagoon to the bend in the channel along an east to west run including 6 points (F1, E1, D1, C1, B1, and A1) and (2) from the bend in the channel to West Pond along a north to south run of 12 points (A1 to A12). In addition, 3 to 5 points were determined perpendicular to the flow at each transect point. These secondary points

were spaced approximately 15 m apart (i.e. D0.5, D1.5 and
D2.0) (Figure 4).

In addition to the swamp reference points, two
stilling wells for tide measurement were established by
setting slotted PVC pipe at the open water in the lagoon
island margins, one at the Twin Cay dock in the channel
separating West Island from East Island (TG1) and one on
the open lagoon shore at the west side of West Island
(TG1).

Water level and water depth measurements were made by
periodic tape measurements from the tops of the pipes and
elevations of water surface and ground were calculated
based on the reference datum. Additionally, continuous
water level data at five locations were obtained using
two automated data loggers equipped with pressure
transducers.

Flows were determined at three locations in the
channel. These cross-sections bound two channel
reaches: Reach A by cross-sections at survey points A1
and D1 and Reach B by cross-sections at survey points D1
and E1. The measurements were taken during various times
in the tidal cycle using an electromagnetic velocity
meter and standard methods. Velocities were taken at 0.6
to 1.5 meter intervals to provide between 25 and 50
individual measurements in a cross-section.

The flow of water was also observed and evaluated by
use of dye studies. Rhodamine fluorescent dye, a highly
visible, persistent, but non-toxic dye was used. These
dye studies allowed observations of flow path and
dispersion and calculations of flow rates. The dye
movement was observed in the field and dye samples
collected at discrete times for further laboratory
analysis. Low level balloon photography was used to
document the movement and the dispersion of dye as it
moved through the mangrove root system.

RESULTS

The unique hydrologic nature of the mangrove swamp
flow is characterized by a very shallow depth which
averages only about 1/2 meter at low tide to 2/3 meter at
high tide; cross-section areas which change greatly with
fluctuations especially in the area extent of flooding;
and a very high degree of frictional resistance caused by
the dense tangle of mangrove roots and the ill defined
bottom sediments. Figure 5 shows a typical cross-section
and the relationships of water level to the mangrove
structure.

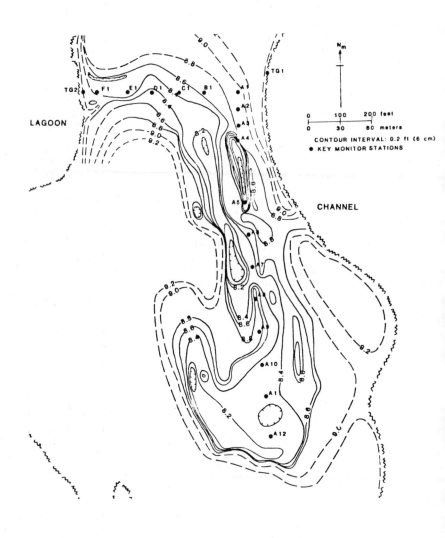

FIGURE 4.   Two principle surveying transects (A1-F1 and A1-A12) on
West Island; Twin Cays, Belize.

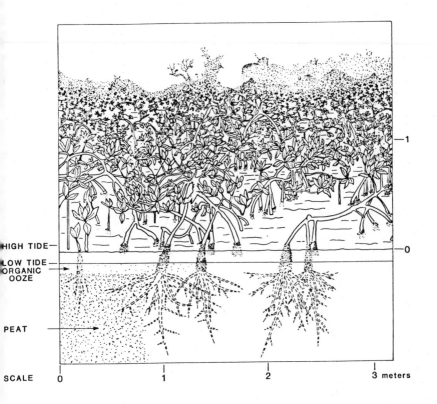

FIGURE 5.   Typical cross-section indicating the relationships of
            water level to the mangrove structure. (Drawn by Molly
            K. Ryan.)

The topography and hydrography of the flooded area is detailed in Figure 4. The highly irregular nature of the bottom is evident by inspection of the contour patterns. Some depressions exist which are as deep as 1.5 m, but are not necessarily coherent with the main flow channel. As the region floods more flow channels develop changing the pattern of flow greatly. In addition, if the tide is high enough, other areas in the interior of the island may get direct flooding from the lagoon. The ground elevation of the island ranges from -1.5 m in the main channel of the swamp to +0.3 m relative to the estimated local mean sea level determined during a two week period of observations. A typical cross-section perpendicular to the main channel for survey line A4/B4 (boundary of Reach A) and survey line E (boundary of Reach B) are shown in Figures 6 and 7, respectively. Inspection shows that the flow does not move through a simple single channel during a tidal cycle but through numerous interconnected channels all of which function to a different degree at varying stages of the tide.

A typical distribution of velocity across a section is also shown in Figures 6 and 7. The flow rates were then determined from the field data and the average cross-section velocity was calculated as the composite flow rate divided by the cross-section area.

It is to be noted that the average velocity is reflective of both the tortuous path of flow through the mangroves and the frictional resistance of the mangrove root system and the channel bottom. This resistance was quantified by inverse calculation from the Manning equation:

$$Q = 1/n \ A \ R^{2/3} \ S^{1/2} \qquad (1)$$

where Q is flow in m^3/s; n is the Manning's roughness factor; A is the cross-sectional area in m^2; and S is the slope of the channel in m/m. Figure 8 shows the variation of Manning's number for frictional resistance with flow. The relationship is represented by a straight line when plotted logarithmically. This form may be expressed in general by:

$$\log n = \log a + b(\log) \ Q \qquad (2)$$

where a and b are a regression coefficient and exponent, respectively. Manning's n was also found to vary logarithmically with depth. It is to be noted that Manning's number varies greatly over the tidal cycle. The implication of this is that flow modeling for a mangrove system must incorporate the variation of Manning's number. Table 1 is a summary of the hydraulic

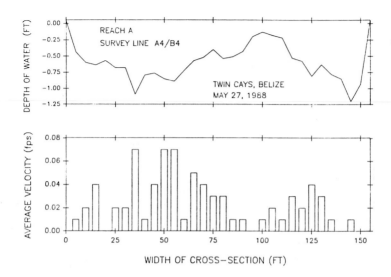

FIGURE 6. Typical channel cross section for survey line A4/B4.

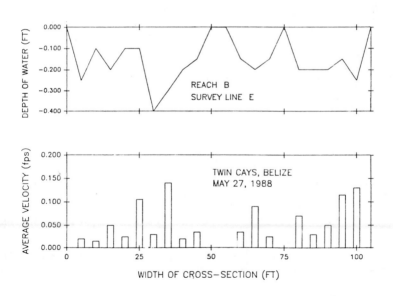

FIGURE 7. Typical channel cross section for survey line E.

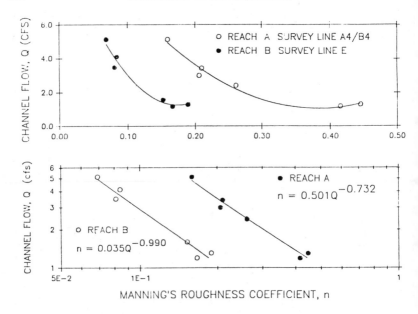

FIGURE 8.   Variation of Manning's roughness factor with flow; top-arithmetic, bottom-logarithmic.

Reach	Obs	Depth (m)	Slope (m/m)	Velocity (m/s)	Flow (cm/s)	n
A	1	0.164	0.000086	0.013	0.097	0.210
	2	0.143	0.000102	0.013	0.085	0.206
	3	0.146	0.000098	0.011	0.069	0.261
	4	0.134	0.000110	0.006	0.037	0.445
	5	0.119	0.000117	0.006	0.034	0.415
	6	0.203	0.000055	0.016	0.145	0.159
B	1	0.076	0.000237	0.004	0.097	0.081
	2	0.066	0.000290	0.018	0.045	0.152
	3	0.095	0.000171	0.034	0.117	0.084
	4	0.067	0.000276	0.015	0.037	0.189
	5	0.057	0.000316	0.016	0.034	0.166
	6	0.115	0.000092	0.034	0.145	0.069

TABLE 1.   Summary of hydraulic parameters.

data determined by reach.

Dye flow studies were made on three different occasions during periods of maximum flow. The dye plume movement was determined both by visual means and by quantitative analysis of the fluorescence in collected samples. This methodology reflects the integrated effect of the multidirectional path of flow through the mangroves as well as the frictional resistance along the flow channel. As might be expected it is less than half the velocity measured as maximum point velocity in the central part of the flow channel and somewhat less than the average velocity determined from cross-section flow analysis.

With respect to tides for the period measured (January 1990) the still water tidal range in the lagoon was about 17.5 cm. At the tide gage set in the mangroves at the edge of the island the tide amplitude was already attenuated to 14.0 cm. However, as the tidal waves up the shallow channel, it is to be noted that there is not a regular attenuation. Rather, the amplitude is modified by the geometry of the hydrologic cross-section, in some instances having a greater amplitude than that in the channel nearer the coast. At the last station, in West Pond where the inflow moves into a broad reservoir, the amplitude is least, being only 9.0 cm as compared with 11.5 cm at the tide gage at the flood channel entrance. The tidal lag time is more predictable, gradually increasing as the tidal wave moves inland. At West Pond a distance of 220 m, the lag time is 4.5 hours. It seems that at times a reflected wave from West Pond interferes or enhances the primary wave moving up the channel.

Since the interior hydrologic system is open directly to the salt water of the lagoon when there is a deficit in the hydrologic budget, i.e. evapo-transpiration greater than precipitation, the deficit in fresh water recharge to the system causes more salt water to move into West Pond to maintain the hydrologic balance. This further exacerbates the situation and creates a hypersaline conditions in the poorly flushed areas. During the wet season when there is more precipitation than evapo-transpiration, the opposite effect occurs with the pond becoming less salty due to dilution of the salt water precipitation.

CONCLUSIONS

The surface hydrology of a Caribbean outwashed mangrove island was investigated. Manning's roughness factor, n, was determined at several locations and found to vary considerably with the tidal cycle. The root structure appeared to significantly attenuate the tidal forced water flow within the inter-island channel.

ACKNOWLEDGMENTS

This study was supported by the Smithsonian Institution and by the Exxon Corporation and is Contribution Number 319 to the Caribbean Coral Reef Ecosystems Program (CCRE) of the Smithsonian Institution.

REFERENCES

Holdridge, L.R. (1940). "Some Notes on the Mangrove Swamps of Puerto Rico." Caribbean, 1, 19-29.
Kjerfve, B., Ruetzler, K., and Kierspe, G.H. (1982). "Tides at Carrie Bow Cay, Belize." Smithsonian Contributions to the Marine Sciences, (12), 47-51.
Lugo, A.E. and Snedaker, S.C. (1974). "The Ecology of Mangroves." Annual Review of Ecology and Systematics, 5, 39-64.
Ruetzler, K. and Macintyre, I.G. (1982). "The Atlantic Barrier Reef Ecosystem at Carrie Bow Cay, Belize,I - Structure and Communities." Smithsonian Contributions to the Marine Sciences, (12), 539pp.
Ruetzler, K. and Feller, C. (1988). "Mangrove Swamp Communities." Oceanus, 30(4), 16-24.

SUBJECT INDEX
Page number refers to first page of paper.

AUTHOR INDEX
Page number refers to first page of paper.